Chabad-Lubavitch
The Lamplighters

Published by
Merkos L'Inyonei Chinuch
770 Eastern Parkway
Brooklyn, New York 11213
5749 - 1988

Merkos L'Inyonei Chinuch
770 Eastern Parkway
Brooklyn, New York 11213

With thanks to
Rabbi Yitschak Meir Kagan
for his invaluable assistance.

Design, layout and art
by Skidmore Sahratian Inc.

ISBN 0-8266-0381-5

Printed in the United States of America

Table Of Contents

Chabad-Lubavitch
The Lamplighters

The "Street-Lamp Lighter"

נר ה׳ נשמת אדם
(משלי כ׳ כ"ז)

*The soul of man
is the candle of G-d.
(Proverbs 20:27)*

"...I was once privileged to hear from my father-in-law (Rabbi Yosef Yitzchak Schneersohn, of saintly memory, the previous Lubavitcher Rebbe) that his father, Rabbi Shalom Dovber, of saintly memory, was once asked, 'What is a Chabad-Lubavitch chassid?'

He replied, 'A chassid is like a street-lamp lighter.' In olden days, there was a person in every town who would light the street-lamps with a light he carried at the end of a long pole. On the street-corners, the lamps were there in readiness, waiting to be lit; sometimes, however, the lamps are not as easily accessible. There are lamps in forsaken places, in deserts, or at sea. There must be someone to light even those lamps, so that they may fulfill their purpose and light up the paths of others.

It is written, 'The soul of man is the candle of G-d.' It is also written, 'A mitzva is a candle, and the Torah is light.' A chassid is one who puts his personal affairs aside and sets out to light up the souls of Jews with the light of Torah and mitzvot. Jewish souls are ready and waiting to be kindled. Sometimes they are close, nearby; sometimes they are in a desert, or at sea. There must be someone who will forgo his or her own comforts and conveniences, and reach out to light those lamps. This is the function of a true Chabad-Lubavitch chassid.

The message is obvious. I will only add that this function is not really limited to chassidim, but is the function of every Jew. Divine Providence brings Jews to the most unexpected, remote places, so that they may carry out this purpose of lighting up the world.

May G-d grant that each and every one of us be a dedicated 'street-lamp lighter,' and fulfill his or her duty with joy and gladness of heart."

*Adapted from an address by the Lubavitcher Rebbe,
Rabbi Menachem M. Schneerson שליט"א, on the 13th day of Tammuz, 5722*

Main Photo:
The Lubavitcher
Rebbe, Rabbi
Menachem Mendel
Schneerson שליט״א.

Foreword

ואהבת לרעך כמוך
(ויקרא יט, יח)

*Love your fellow
as yourself.
(Leviticus 19:18)*

The discussion centered around several simple folk—whom the Rebbe praised effusively.

A diamond merchant, one of the Rebbe's distinguished followers, exclaimed, "Why do you make so much of them?"

The Rebbe: "They possess fine qualities."

The chassid: "I don't see it."

Later, the Rebbe suddenly asked to see the merchant's packet of diamonds.

The chassid spread them out, and pointed to a stone; "This one is a superlatively wonderful gem."

The Rebbe: "I see nothing in it!"

The chassid: "One has to be a *mayvin* (expert)."

The Rebbe: "A Jew is superlatively wonderful—but you have to be a *mayvin!*"

Sefer Hasichot 5705, p. 41.

This is the philosophy of Chabad-Lubavitch, the world's largest Jewish educational outreach organization.

Chabad-Lubavitch is a vibrant, dynamic force in Jewish life, and its programs touch the lives of millions of people and directly or indirectly affect Jewish life in every community.

How many institutions does Chabad-Lubavitch have, what is its program, what services does it provide and who is being served? Who are its workers, representatives and emissaries? What motivates them? This book will provide some answers to those questions. Although some outlines of philosophical background are included, this book's prime focus is on the *activities* of Chabad-Lubavitch. Furthermore, it is only a general overview—an exhaustive study would require volumes.

The Names, "Chabad," "Lubavitch": Chabad Chassidism is a system of Jewish religious philosophy which teaches understanding and recognition of the Creator and the role and purpose of creation through the application of the three intellectual qualities of *chochma* ("wisdom"), *bina* ("comprehension"), and *daat* ("knowledge"). The initials of these three Hebrew words form the word *Chabad.*

For over a century, the movement was centered in the town of Lubavitch in White Russia. Appropriately, the word "Lubavitch" in Russian means the "city of brotherly love." A name is much more than merely a title—it reveals the essence. *Lubavitch has remained ever-faithful to its roots, displaying, above all, an unconditional love for every Jew.*

Kislev 14, 5749

"Lubavitch has remained ever-faithful to its roots, displaying, above all, an unconditional love for every Jew."

The Rebbe

הנשיא הוא הכל

(רש״י במדבר כ״א, כ״א)

*The leader is (as)
all (the people).
(Rashi,
Numbers 21:21)*

The Lubavitcher Rebbe, Rabbi Menachem M. Schneerson *sh'lita*,* is the seventh leader in the Lubavitch-Chabad dynasty. He has been described as the most phenomenal Jewish personality of our time. To his hundreds of thousands of followers and millions of sympathizers and admirers around the world, he is "the Rebbe," today's most dominant figure in Judaism and, undoubtedly, the one individual more than any other singularly responsible for stirring the conscience and spiritual awakening of world Jewry.

Born in 1902, on the 11th day of Nissan, in Nikolaev, Russia, the Rebbe is the son of the renowned kabbalist and talmudic scholar, the late Rabbi Levi Yitzchak Schneerson, and Rebbetzin Chana. He is the great-grandson—and namesake—of the third Rebbe, Rabbi Menachem Mendel of Lubavitch. (His mother, Rebbetzin Chana, 1880-1964, during her famous husband's exile by the Soviets to a remote village in Asian Russia, displayed legendary courage and ingenuity; for example, she labored to make inks from herbs she gathered in the fields—so that Rabbi Levi Yitzchak could continue writing his commentary on *kabbala* and other Torah-subjects.)

To Save a Life: There is a story told about the Rebbe's early life that seems to be almost symbolic of everything that was to follow. When he was nine years old, the young Menachem Mendel courageously dove into the Black Sea and saved the life of a little boy who had fallen from the deck of a moored ship. That sense of "other lives in danger" seems to have dominated his consciousness ever since; of Jews drowning in assimilation, ignorance or alienation—and no one hearing their cries for help; Jews on campus, in isolated communities, under repressive regimes. From early childhood he displayed a prodigious mental acuity. By the time he reached his

Main Photo:
10 Sh'vat, 1987 (5747):
*A farbrengen
(chassidic gathering)
conducted by the
Rebbe at World Luba-
vitch Headquarters,
770 Eastern Parkway,
Brooklyn, New York.*

Main Photo:
19 Kislev, 1954 (5714):
The Rebbe delivers a
maamar—an original,
profound dissertation
of chassidic teach-
ings, while the circle of
elders and senior
rabbis stand in respect.
From left to right:
Rabbi Shmaryahu
Gourary, son-in-law
of the Previous Rebbe;
Rabbi Mordechai
Mentlick, Rabbi
Shmuel Levitin,
the Rebbe (seated at
microphone), Rabbi
Nissan Telushkin,
Rabbi Efrayim Yolles,
Rabbi Shlomo Aron
Kazarnovsky (lower),
Rabbi Berel Rivkin,
Rabbi Mordechai
Hodakov (lower),
Rabbi Mendel Cunin.

*"With the Rebbe
at its helm, Lubavitch
has rapidly grown
to be a worldwide pres-
ence, and all its
various activities are
stamped with
his vision."*

were opened in dozens of cities and university campuses around the world.

Uniqueness: With the Rebbe at its helm, Lubavitch has rapidly grown to be a worldwide presence, and all its various activities are stamped with his vision; small wonder then, that many ask, "What is there about his leadership that is so unique? Why do leading personalities of the day have such profound respect and admiration for him?"

Past, Present, Future: Many leaders recognize the need of the moment and respond with courage and direction. This is *their* forte—an admirable one. Others, though their strength may not lie in "instant response" to current problems, are blessed with the ability of perceptive foresight— knowing what tomorrow will bring and how to best prepare. Still other leaders excel in yet a third distinct area, possessing a keen sense of history and tradition; their advice and leadership is molded by a great sensitivity to the *past.*

But one who possesses all three qualities is truly unique, standing alone in leadership. Such is the Lubavitcher Rebbe—the inspiration and driving force behind the success of Lubavitch today. Radiating a keen sense of urgency, demanding much from his followers, and even more from himself, the Rebbe leads, above all else, *by example.*

Initiation, Not Reaction: He is a rare blend of prophetic visionary and pragmatic leader, synthesizing deep insight into the present needs of the Jewish people with a breadth of vision for its future. In a sense, he charts the course of Jewish history—initiating, in addition to reacting to, current events. The Rebbe is guided by inspired insight and foresight in combination with encyclo- pedic scholarship, and all his pronouncements and undertakings are, first and foremost, rooted in our Holy Torah. Time and again, it has been demonstrated that what was clear to him

Bar Mitzva, the Rebbe was considered an *illuy,* a Torah prodigy. He spent his teen years immersed in the study of Torah.

Marriage in Warsaw: In 1929 Rabbi Menachem Mendel married the previous Rebbe's daughter, Rebbetzin Chaya Moussia, in Warsaw. (The Rebbetzin, born in 1901, was chosen by her father, the Previous Rebbe, to accompany him in his forced exile to Kostroma in 1927. For sixty years she was the wife of the Rebbe; she passed away on Sh'vat 22 in 1988.) He later studied in the University of Berlin and then at the Sorbonne in Paris. It may have been in these years that his formidable knowledge of mathematics, medicine and the sciences began to blossom.

Arrival in the U.S.A.: On Monday, Sivan 28, 5701 (June 23, 1941) the Rebbe and the Rebbetzin arrived in the U.S., having been miraculously rescued, by the grace of Almighty G-d, from the European holocaust. The day marks the launching of sweeping new efforts in bolstering and disseminating Torah and Judaism in general, and chassidic teachings in particular, through the establishment

of three central Lubavitch organizations under the Rebbe's leadership: *Merkos L'Inyonei Chinuch* ("Central Organization For Jewish Education"), *Kehot Publication Society,* and *Machne Israel,* a social services agency. Shortly after his arrival the Rebbe began writing his notations to various chassidic and kabbalistic treatises, as well as a wide range of responsa on Torah subjects. With publication of these works his genius was soon recognized by scholars throughout the world.

Leadership: In 1950, Rabbi Menachem M. Schneerson reluctantly ascended to the leadership of the Lubavitch movement, whose headquarters were—and still are—at 770 Eastern Parkway in Brooklyn, New York. Soon Lubavitch institutions and activities took on new dimensions. The outreaching philosophy of Chabad-Lubavitch was translated into action, as Lubavitch centers and Chabad Houses

A.

B.

C.

*A. Rabbi Levi
Yitzchak Schneerson
of blessed memory,
1878-1944, father of
the Rebbe sh'lita.*
*B. The Rebbe in
the 1950s.*
*C. The Rebbe, in the
1940s, supporting his
father-in-law—the
Previous Lubavitcher
Rebbe, Rabbi Yosef
Yitzchak Schneersohn,
of blessed memory,
1880-1950.*
*Inset below:
The Rebbe officiating
at a wedding in 1958.*

*Main Photo:
Leaving his house on
President Street,
the Rebbe acknowl-
edges the greetings
of a young child.*

at the outset became obvious to other leaders with hindsight, decades later.

Everyone's Unique Role: From the moment the Rebbe arrived in America in 1941, his brilliance at addressing himself to the following ideal became apparent: He would not acknowledge division or separation. Every Jew—indeed every human being—has a unique role to play in the greater scheme of things and is an integral part of the tapestry of G-d's creation.

For nearly five of the most critical decades in recent history, the Rebbe's plan to reach out to every corner of the world with love and concern has continued to unfold dramatically. No sector of the community has been excluded—young and old; men and women; leader and layman; scholar and laborer; student and teacher; children, and even infants.

He has an uncanny ability to meet everyone at their own level—advising Heads of State on matters of national and international importance, exploring with professionals the complexities in their own fields of expertise, and talking to small children with warm words and a fatherly smile.

"Actualize Your Potential!" With extraordinary insight, he perceives the wealth of potential in each person. His inspiration boosts the individual's self-perception, ignites his awareness of that hidden wealth and motivates a desire to fulfill his potential. In the same way, many a community has been transformed by the Rebbe's message, and been given—directly or indirectly—a new sense of purpose and confidence. In each encounter the same strong, if subtle message is imparted: "You are Divinely gifted with enormous strength and energy—actualize it!"

May the Almighty, who has blessed our generation with this unique beacon of light—the Rebbe *sh'lita*—bestow His blessings upon the Rebbe for long, healthy years, and may we merit the ultimate redemption with the advent of *Mashiach* (the Messiah) speedily, in our days.

"YEAR OF BUILDING" LAUNCHED

In September and October 1988, before the onset of the Jewish new year 5749—and continuing into the new year, the Rebbe called for a "Year of Building," an unprecedented campaign of construction, acquisition and expansion of buildings housing Chabad-Lubavitch institutions and activities.

On the eve of Elul 18, "Chai Elul," 5748 (August 30, 1988) the Rebbe personally participated in ground-breaking for the new World Headquarters synagogue and building at 770 Eastern Parkway in Brooklyn, New York.

Traditionally, the foundation-stone is an unhewn, natural rock placed into the ground and covered with earth.

(photos and captions on facing page)

A.

B.

C.

THE REBBE BREAKS GROUND— WORLDWIDE:

Eve of "Chai Elul," 5748, (August 30, 1988). Ground-breaking for the new World Headquarters at 770 Eastern Parkway in Brooklyn, N.Y. launches the "Year of Building" around the world.

A. Placing the unhewn natural rock into the ground, to serve as the foundation-stone for the new building.
B. Covering the foundation-stone with earth. At the Rebbe's left is Mr. David T. Chase, Chairman of the 770 Building Committee.
C. Following the ground-breaking, the Rebbe addresses a crowd of some ten thousand persons, and explains the Jewish concepts of "ground-breaking" and "foundation-stone," and their significance.

Distinguished visitors to the Rebbe:
A. *Hagaon Rav Yosef Dov Soloveitchik at a public farbrengen.*
B. *Menachem Begin meets the Rebbe during his first visit to the United States as Prime Minister, to hear the Rebbe's views and receive his blessings.*
C. *The late Zalman Shazar, President of Israel, at the head-table of a farbrengen*
D. *Herman Wouk, at the head-table of a major farbrengen.*

ON THIS SITE WILL BE ERECTED

BETH CHAYA MUSHKA SCHNEERSOHN

בית חי' מושקא שניאורסאהן

שמחת אם בישראל

נדר יחי' כבוד חבית הוד

ליובאוויטש – הרבנית הצדקנית

INTERNATIONAL EDUCATION CAMPUS BETH RIVKA SCHOOLS

מרכז חינוך עולמי דבית רבקה

LUBAVITCH, IN MEMORY OF OUR REVERED REBETZIN

*Ground-breaking
for the new ten-million
dollar campus for the
Beth Rivkah Girls'
Schools in Brooklyn,
New York, to serve
1500 girls enrolled in
the schools. The
campus is named for
Rebbetzin Chaya
Mushka Schneerson,
O.B.M., 1901-1988,
wife of the Rebbe.
Inset: U.S. industrial-
ist Ronald O. Perelman,
benefactor of the
new campus project,
speaking at the event.*

We Are One

*The second soul
of a Jew is truly part
of G-d above.
(Tanya, Ch. 2)*

Once upon a time there were different synagogues for different social classes; one synagogue for carpenters and shoemakers, another for farmers, and an entirely separate one for learned Torah-scholars, who would not pray alongside the "common folk."

Unbelievable? Just two hundred years ago, throughout the *shtetls* of Eastern Europe, such was indeed the situation.

Then came the Baal Shem Tov.

Rabbi Israel Baal Shem Tov (lit. "Master of the Good Name"; 1694-1748), founder of Chassidism, showed how such "social" divisions were inimical to Judaism. He explained the common Divine origin of *all* souls, and the beautiful traits of spiritual treasures to be found in every Jew, whether scholarly or unlearned. He taught:

It is written, "For you (the Jewish People) shall be a land of desire, says the L-rd of Hosts."

Just as the greatest scientists will never discover the limits of the enormous natural resources which the Almighty has sunk into the land, neither will anyone ever find the limits of the great treasures which lie within Yisrael—G-d's "land of desire."

Everywhere he went, the Baal Shem Tov broke down the barriers between Jews, building bridges of *ahavat yisrael* (love of one's fellow), bringing them together, teaching them about their enormous obligations of mutual responsibility and mutual affection; showing that *we are one.*

But opposition was fierce—sometimes fanatical. Building bridges between the Torah-scholar and the unlettered—declared his opponents—degraded the honor of Torah and encouraged simplicity.

Yet, within several generations, the chassidic attitude became universal. In our own age, the notion of separate synagogues for different classes of Jews seems such an absurdity that some,

Main Photo:
*The Torah-scroll is
held high for all to see.
There are 600,000
letters in the Torah,
and of the Jews present
at the Giving of
Torah on Mount Sinai,
there were 600,000
"representative
essential souls." Each
and every one of
our people "has his or
her letter" in the Torah;
through Torah,*
we are one.

to this very day, find it difficult to accept that the Baal Shem Tov was indeed the author of the barrier-melting revolution in Jewish society two centuries ago.

History repeats itself. Just seventy or eighty years ago, all smaller rural communities throughout Europe consisted entirely of religious people; a non-observant Jew was an unheard-of phenomenon. But the subsequent upheaval of two World Wars utterly changed the face of Jewish society, and in the 1930s and 1940s we find the communities of Western Europe and America divided into two separate, distinct camps—partially or totally non-religious in one group, and the observant in the other, with the latter having no desire to mix with, or to reach out to, the non-religious camp. Then came Lubavitch, in the 1940s, and the assault on the barricades dividing Jew from Jew began in earnest.

Inset, below:
Offering a passerby
the opportunity to
participate in the obser-
vance of etrog
and lulav on the Sukot
festival, in Melbourne,
Australia.

First and foremost, Lubavitch pioneered the day-school system in America, introducing the concept that a full-time Torah-education be made available for *all* Jewish children. Then they turned their attention to the Public Schools, where the majority of Jewish children in attendance were non-religious. Yet, precisely for those children, Lubavitch educators utilized the "Released Time" provision of New York State Law to set up, in 1942, a network of classes providing basic Torah-instruction for one hour a week. "Mesibos Shabbos" youth groups for Shabbat afternoons were established; Chabad chassidim began to appear on the city streets during the *Sukot* festival, offering *etrog* and *lulav,* to whom?—to the unobservant, of course; the first Torah-oriented English children's monthly in the world, "Talks and Tales," first came off the press for Chanuka, 1942 (and has continued uninterrupted publication up to the present, for 47 years, now throughout the world in many languages).

Thirty years ago, Russian-born "chabadniks" sat shoulder to shoulder with their Jewish brothers of supposedly doctrinaire communistic and "anti-religious" persuasion, in an atmosphere of warm affection and joyous friendship, at a chassidic gathering in the Israeli Lubavitch settlement of Kfar Chabad. The world's first *yeshiva* for *baalei teshuva* ("returnees" to Jewish practice), Hadar Hatorah, opened its doors in Brooklyn in 1962; later, another, the *Tiferes Bachurim* "New Direction Program" in Morristown, New Jersey. Then the Chabad Houses...

...And the rest is history.

Just as in the Baal Shem Tov's era, the Lubavitch barrier-breaking approach was, at first, sharply criticized, even attacked with vehemence; and once again, after the passage of only a few years, the Jewish day-school system and an "outreach attitude" has become all-but-universal. Throughout the community it is becoming increasingly recognized and accepted that we are one. A oneness unique to the Jewish people. Limbs of the same body. Strengthening one limb, one Jew, fortifies us all. A oneness given frequent and eloquent emphasis within Chabad Chassidism, reflecting its fundamental belief that every Jew, regardless of affiliation or background, possesses a *neshama,* a unique soul, a G-dly spark. In its essence, this spark of G-dliness is common to all Jews and equal in all Jews, which gives new significance to the often-repeated colloquialism, "A Jew is a Jew is a Jew."

By virtue of the *neshama,* the Torah and all its precepts are the inheritance, the right and the privilege of all our people. So when the question is raised, "Why do you put on *tefillin* in the street, or hand out Shabbat candles and candleholders, to men and women whom you have never met before?" the *chassid* of Lubavitch responds:

Inset, below:
A newborn baby proudly displays the emblem showing her to be a member of "G-d's Army" of children (Tzivos Hashem).

Because of what they already are, not because of what they may become; not so that he or she may one day become "orthodox," but because right now they are already Jewish, and tefillin and Shabbat-candles belong to them; it is their right and their obligation to perform the mitzva, and it is our privilege, honor and obligation to respectfully help them do so, with the same fervor and compassion that I would provide a warm meal and a place to sleep for a passerby whom I have never seen before and may never see again.

Some have termed outreach *kiruv rechokim,* "drawing close those who are distant."

Lubavitch comments: No Jew should be characterized as "distant," for, in essence, *we are one.*

Rabbi Schneur Zalman of Liadi, founder of Chabad-Lubavitch declared: "Grandfather (as he called the Baal Shem Tov) deeply loved simple folk. In my first days in Mezritch, my Rebbe (the Baal Shem Tov's successor) said: *It was a frequent customary remark of the Baal Shem Tov that love of Yisrael is love of G-d. "You are children of G-d your G-d"; when one loves the father— one loves the children.*

Hayom Yom, Av 24.

"No Jew should be characterized as 'distant,' for, in essence, we are one."

Inset, below: Distributing food for Passover to needy Russian immigrants.

Main Photo:
A family receives
Purim food-gifts
(mishlo'ach manot)
from Rabbi Mordechai
Kanelsky.

22

The Sh'liach—
The Emissary

שלוחו של אדם כמותו
(ברכות לד, ב)

*One's emissary
is as oneself.*
(Brachot 34b)

They are a team. Husband and wife. *Sh'liach* and *sh'lucha*. They are emissaries of the Rebbe,

the respresentatives of Lubavitch, the messengers of Chabad.

They are the *sh'luchim.*

Within the Lubavitch community, the title *sh'liach* evokes respect, perhaps even a tinge of envy.

They are the chosen few, the elite. Children aspire to be *sh'luchim,* dreaming of manning a Chabad

House in far-off exotic lands where strange languages are spoken. The product of childish minds,

it is an idealized dream, free of the difficulties and traumas that beset the *sh'liach* in real life.

There are no trumpets sounded when they arrive in their new home city; no red carpets unrolled

in their honor. They have few friends, no relatives, no familiar culture, atmosphere or environment.

Many commodities, such as kosher meat, dairy products and other basics, may have to be

flown in, but there are certain staples, vitally essential to their mission, which they bring with them

by the truckload: Friendliness, affection for *all* Jews, compassion, tolerance, self-sacrifice,

utter devotion and selfless dedication.

Armed with these, they immediately begin their work of outreach—explaining, shedding light,

dispelling myths, countering stereotypes. "What does it mean to be a Jew?" "Rabbi, how can I observe

Shabbat—when my store has its best sales on Saturday?" "How are mitzvot relevant *today,*

in *this* community?" The *sh'liach* of Chabad does not insist; he suggests. He does not criticize;

he encourages. He does not "preach down" at people, but acts as a genuine *equal,* a friend.

And the revolution begins.

It takes place without anyone realizing it. A few years fly by, and, "out of nowhere,"

it is a familiar and accepted sight to see families with *sukot,* observing Shabbat, *kashrut,* etc. ...

Main Photo:
*International Convention of sh'luchim,
Tevet 5, 5748;
December 26, 1987,
in front of World
Lubavitch Headquarters, 770 Eastern Parkway, Brooklyn, N.Y.
(It should be noted
that the delegates
pictured here are
only representatives
of the overall body
of sh'luchim—many
of whom were
unable to attend the
Convention).*

Beyond The Jewish Community

והלכו גוים לאורך ומלכים
לנוגה זרחך
(ישעי׳ ס. ג)

*Nations shall walk
by your light, and
kings by the brightness
of your shine.
(Isaiah 60:3)*

*A. A veteran sh'liach:
Rabbi Nissan Pinson
of Tunisia, with some
pupils at the Chabad
school in Tunis.
B. A sh'liach arrives:
Rabbi Yosef
Y. Weingarten is wel-
comed at the airport
of the small Jewish
community of Grand
Rapids, Michigan,
September 1977.
C. Ten years later:
The spacious new
Chabad House of
Grand Rapids arises.
Inset, below:
Convention of the
sh'luchim in Latin
America.*

For the longest time, man has been experimenting with a variety of ideologies,

ostensibly to establish a truly civilized world in which he can live with purpose and in happiness.

The condition of the world today, however, bears testimony to his pathetic failure.

Human logic alone simply cannot formulate a system of ethics and morality that will be universally

acceptable and binding.

Witnessing the moral degeneracy of today's society, what should the Jewish response be?

Perhaps we should withdraw and become an isolationist community, concerned only with our own

survival and developing our "chosenness" solely to our own advantage? That might indeed

serve our own interests to a degree, but it has always been a key component of G-d's plan that we,

the People of Torah, should share with mankind the way towards hope and purpose.

No, Judaism is not a proselytizing religion. It does not seek converts. We believe that every

person has a mission to fulfill in G-d's creation, and can be deemed worthy of the Almighty's rewards—

both in This World and in The World To Come—providing, of course, that he or she accepts

and follows the guidelines that have been Divinely ordained for him or her. For the Jew, this means

the 613 commandments. For the non-Jew—i.e. all "descendants of Noah"—it means the basic

program of ethical monotheism built on seven commandments, the universal moral code called

"The Seven Laws for the Descendants of Noah."

"The Seven Noahide Laws" begin with the prohibition against worship of anything but the

One Supreme G-d, and contain an orderly system of ethical behavior, comprising the code by which

all of mankind is obligated to live. The Rebbe has launched a campaign to teach and disseminate

the Noahide Code to the world at large.

Main Photo:
President Reagan
signs a proclamation
honoring the Rebbe
for his efforts on behalf
of education in general,
and disseminating
the Universal Noahide
Code in particular.
Left to right:
Rabbis Yisroel Deren
(Stamford, Connect-
icut), Moshe Feller
(Minnesota), Shlomo
Cunin (California),
the President, Rabbis
Avraham Shemtov
(Philadelphia, Penn-
sylvania), Shimon
Lazaroff (Texas),
Yakov Kranz
(Virginia).

There is an obvious question, "Why now?" Why embark upon this outreach program to the Gentiles at this particular time in history? Why have the great Torah-leaders of previous generations not appeared to consider this a priority? The answer is, that throughout his turbulent history, with very few exceptions, the Jew has not been in a position to communicate on this level with his non-Jewish neighbor. The Jew has been a victim of severe circumstances, and could not dare suggest that he had something to teach his contemptuous hosts about faith and morality.

Today, in most countries, the Jew is, thank G-d, free to speak his mind on almost every subject. He would therefore be failing in his religious obligation and moral duty were he to choose to be an "unconcerned bystander" and not share his knowledge and insights with others.

The opportunity triggers the obligation.

The obligation, in turn, triggers action—which has been highly successful on two levels, the governmental and the grass-roots. Some examples: Heads of State and government officials of various countries—particularly the United States—have issued proclamations encouraging their citizens to observe the Noahide moral code. At the grass-roots level, a host of successful programs include a video tape for ethical instruction in the public school classroom.

Professionally produced in 1987 by the Lubavitch Foundation of London, England, this video presentation has been highly acclaimed by British educators, and has been used in hundreds of schools in England and the United States.

History repeats itself. As with many of the Rebbe's past campaigns, the initial sense of "innovation" was total. The average non-Jew, though familiar with the Ten Commandments, had never heard of the Seven Noahide Laws. Yet now, only a few years after the

"...it has always been a key component of G-d's plan that we, the People of Torah, should share with mankind the way towards hope and purpose."

Inset, below: Motti Feldman, age 15, listens to the Rt. Hon. Bob Hawke, Prime Minister of Australia, after having explained the Noahide Laws to him; Parliament House, Canberra, Australia.

Main Photo:
Presentation to the Rt.
Hon. Martin Brian
Mulroney, Prime
Minister of Canada.
Left to right:
Rabbi Zalman A.
Grossbaum (Ontario),
Rabbi Berel Mockin
(Lubavitch Youth
Organization,
Montreal, Quebec),
Professor Yitschak
Block (London,
Ontario), Rabbi
Avraham Altein
(Winnipeg, Manitoba).

Inset, below:
Presentation of a
menora to President
Reagan.

launching of the campaign, leaders in both government and education around the world are making increasing mention of the Noahide Laws as a cardinal foundation for ethical behavior. Seriously concerned by the erosion of morality all around them, they express warm appreciation of, and support for, the campaign.

Within the Jewish community, too, there is a greatly heightened awareness of the obligation to utilize one's contacts with non-Jewish friends and acquaintances not only for material concerns but also to impart moral influence, to inform and educate about the Noahide Laws.

In summary: What is the Chabad-Lubavitch attitude to the non-Jewish world? Just this; that if we live our lives with Divine dignity and purpose, we will inevitably inspire others; if we talk about a Supreme Being who created this world and continues to watch over it, others will begin to sense His presence; and if we vociferously deny vulgarity and promote G-d-given decency and purposefulness, others will follow our example. In these times of moral crisis, an all-out attempt must be made to remind all people of their original purpose. The ultimate intention of G-d's plan will be realized when *everyone* declares this world to be G-d Almighty's dwelling-place, and recognizes that, "The earth and all in it is the L-rd's, the world and all its inhabitants." *Psalm 24.*

Inset, below: Explaining the seven Noahide Laws to the secretary of the King of Swaziland, Africa.

Main Photos:
Upper: The Hon. Jose Sarney, President of the Republic of Brazil signs the international scroll of honor in tribute to the Rebbe. Left to right: Rabbi Avraham Shemtov, President Sarney, Rabbi Shabse Alpern, Rabbi Yakov Chazan.
Lower: Rabbi Yehuda Leib Raskin explains Lubavitch activities and the Noahide Laws to the Hon. Mr. Afifi, Assistant Prime Minister of Morocco.

International Scroll of Honor

presented by the Heads of State of a grateful World
in tribute to the vision and spiritual leadership provided by
the Lubavitcher Rebbe

Rabbi Menachem Mendel Schneerson שליט״א

on the occasion of his reaching the
EIGHTY-FIFTH YEAR

Whereas, the Lubavitcher Rebbe, Rabbi Menachem M. Schneerson, has reached the
eighty-fifth year of his life which is devoted to the service of world Jewry and
humanity in general; and

Whereas, his venerated vision, wisdom and leadership have contributed greatly
to the promotion of education and the betterment of mankind by his call to recognize
the historical tradition of ethical values and principles which have been the bedrock
of society from the dawn of civilization when they were known as the Seven Noahide
Laws, transmitted through G-d to Moses on Mount Sinai; and

Whereas, the Lubavitcher movement, through its scores of educational centers in
this country and abroad dedicates itself to the preservation, protection and fostering
of these universal values that all men hold true; and

Whereas, the President and both houses of Congress of the United States of
America have accordingly recognized "Education Day - U.S.A." and "National Day
of Reflection" on his birthday, and similar recognition offered by other nations on
this day; now, therefore, be it

Resolved, on the occasion of his birthday, April 10, 1987 corresponding to the
11th of Nissan 5747, we the undersigned do present the Lubavitcher Rebbe,
Rabbi Menachem Mendel Schneerson שליט״א the International Scroll of Honor
recognizing his brilliant achievements and wishing him health, long life and many
more years of leadership to crown his celebrated career.

Ronald Reagan

THE WHITE HOUSE

WASHINGTON

November 20, 1987

It is a pleasure to send greetings to everyone
gathered with Rabbi Menachem Schneerson and the
Merkos L'Inyonei Chinuch. The representation of
the Lubavitch movement in so many countries is
testimony to the power and strength of its ideas.

I recently had the honor of signing the International
Scroll of Honor that pays tribute to Rabbi Schneerson
and affirms fundamental ethical values upon which
all civilized societies must be based. I know that
those of you gathered this week at Lubavitch World
Headquarters promote the acceptance of the Almighty's
commandments to all mankind. In doing so, you
combat the antireligious forces that have caused so
much misery in our lifetimes. I applaud your work.

You have my best wishes for a successful meeting
and for the future.

Ronald Reagan

34

Tzivos Hashem; G-d's Army Of Children

מפי עוללים ויונקים יסדת עוז

(תהילים ח, ג)

Out of the mouths of babes and sucklings you have ordained strength. (Psalms 8:3)

In the Autumn of 1980, the Rebbe unfurled his vision of a new educational campaign for Jewish children.

He asked that an organization be formed, exclusively for boys under the age of bar-mitzva (13), and girls under the age of bat-mitzva (12), to be called *Tzivos Hashem*—"The Army of G-d." Perhaps the Rebbe desired to bolster the spiritual "lines of defense" of the Jewish people, by mustering an army of children and drawing on their enthusiasm and sincerity to lay the foundations for a Jewish tomorrow.

When a child is born into this world, all its impulses and behavior are basically self-centered. It wants to eat, and sleep, and receive its mother's love; *giving* is a concept which is not yet within its grasp. Our sages tell us that although a newborn infant has a G-dly soul, that soul has not yet been internalized in such a way as to influence its behavior. Only gradually does the soul begin to manifest itself in the child's personality. This is the process of education—learning to express oneself, to care for others, to cooperate and share, to grow from being self-centered toward the fulfillment of "Love your fellow as yourself"—that all-embracing mitzva which Rabbi Akiva calls the "great general principle of the Torah."

Despite all the advances of modern civilization, the quality of education in today's world leaves much to be desired. Instead of promoting the growth of caring, sensitive, loving children, contemporary culture often glorifies selfishness, arrogance, and cunning; and society's educational institutions are increasingly ineffective in their efforts to counteract this trend. Violence in the schools, vandalism, insubordination, and the all-pervasive drug culture

"This is the process
of education—
learning to express
oneself, to care
for others, to cooper-
ate and share."

are symptoms of a tragic failure in education. It has become a matter of great concern, not only to educators at large, but also—and even more so—to Jewish educators.

Quality Torah-education for all children has always been a top priority in the Chabad-Lubavitch movement. For generations, its leaders have been a powerful force in the establishment of innovative, effective educational institutions, and have been a source of inspiration to educators and parents throughout the world. It was in keeping with this tradition that Tzivos Hashem was founded.

Around the world, the idea of Tzivos Hashem caught on like wildfire. From the intensely observant, to those with minimal background, tens of thousands of children warmly embraced the idea of being in "G-d's Army." Using the idea of "ranks," the children are instructed how they could earn promotions by doing mitzvot, observing holidays, caring for others in need, showing qualities of respect, cleanliness, honesty, and helpfulness.

"...the idea of Tzivos Hashem caught on like wildfire. From the intensely observant, to those with minimal background... children warmly embraced the idea of being in "G-d's Army."

In the few short years since its establishment, Tzivos Hashem has become the largest Jewish youth organization in America, with more than 125,000 members. Internationally, the numbers have exceeded half a million, making Tzivos Hashem the largest and most vibrant Jewish youth group in the world. Needless to say, education is not limited to the hours a child is in school. In fact, one of the basic concepts behind Tzivos Hashem is the notion that boys and girls should be good "soldiers" twenty-four hours a day. The "army" motif is a superb means for arousing children's natural enthusiasm. The army's aims are, of course, entirely peaceful. Its "armaments" and strategies are kindness and good deeds, prayer and Torah study. And the "enemy" against whom its members wage war is the *yetzer hara*—the inner inclination toward selfish or bad behavior.

500,000 members: "Internationally, the numbers have exceeded half a million, making Tzivos Hashem the largest and most vibrant Jewish youth group in the world."

38

In Israel, where children have no school in the afternoon, regular Tzivos Hashem "rallies" draw literally thousands of children off the streets, in every one of the communities reached by Chabad.

Throughout Europe and North Africa, in England, France, Austria, Holland, Italy, Spain, and Morocco, children of all ages are being trained by Chabad rabbis with Central Headquarters in New York serving as a source of valuable ideas and guidance.

In South America, Tzivos Hashem groups are active in cities and towns throughout Brazil, Venezuela, Peru, Uruguay, Argentina, Colombia, Chile, and even high in the mountains of Bolivia.

Moving towards the east, enthusiastic "Field Reports" of Tzivos Hashem activities continue to arrive from the regiments in South Africa (3,000), Australia (10,000) and even from a Tzivos Hashem outpost in Hong Kong.

No one had dreamed just how dynamic an impact Tzivos Hashem was to have.

No one except the Rebbe, who had again shown such vision and profound understanding of the requirements of our times.

"...Field Reports of Tzivos Hashem activities continue to arrive from the regiments in South Africa, Australia and even from an outpost in Hong Kong."

Keeping in Touch: When a boy or girl first signs up in Tzivos Hashem, they are welcomed to the ranks with a Newsletter explaining the goals of a child in "Hashem's Army," an "Update" of some twenty "Mitzva Missions" to work on, a Tzivos Hashem badge, wallet, ID number, and a copy of the "Twelve Torah Passages" for Jewish children to memorize. As each holiday approaches, another Newsletter arrives, with new information, stories, reports from the children themselves, and more Mitzva Missions to fulfill. In addition, Tzivos Hashem publishes a bi-monthly, "The Moshiach Times," featuring top writers and world-famous artists

(Dave Berg, Joe Kubert, Al Jaffee). The Moshiach Times is also translated and reproduced
in England, Italy, Brazil (in Portuguese), and in Spanish in Venezuela, Chile, Argentina, Uruguay,
Spain and Colombia. Tzivos Hashem uniforms instill pride in many of these communities.

A leader in innovative Jewish education, Tzivos Hashem has produced and developed a host
of educational toys, books, and games, and its New York bookstore is a central clearing house for
high quality educational materials, from hundreds of manufacturers, for schools, camps,
bookstores, and giftshops.

Innovative ideas shape young minds: In 1988, for example, a brilliant new step in education was
taken with the launching of a "birthday awareness" campaign. The child (or his parents) is encouraged
to invite friends to come and celebrate, in a Torah spirit of camaraderie, his or her "specialness"
as a unique individual and his or her attaining another year of growth—spiritually as well as physically.
The Jewish Birthday Club of Tzivos Hashem promotes this concept, and gets the youngsters
thinking about the day they set out on their special mission in life.

"**D**ial a Jewish Story," produced by legendary radio personality Himan Brown, now boasts
a library of 200 tapes and is syndicated in more than 100 cities.

In the large urban centers, Tzivos Hashem reaches out to its sizeable audience with a weekly
radio program (more than 350 consecutive shows), as well as mitzva contests, carnivals, concerts,
expositions and festival rallies that attract tens of thousands of children.

In the winter of 1988, the "Jewish Children's Expo" at the Jacob Javits Convention Center
in Manhattan drew 89,000 children to a kaleidoscope of Jewish history and tradition.

But Tzivos Hashem is also the intimate meeting of a child and his mentor, a boy from a non-affiliated

"...a brilliant new step in education was taken with the launching of a "birthday awareness" campaign."

*Inset, below:
At the Jewish Children's Expo in New York's Convention Center, a youngster signs up for membership in Tzivos Hashem.*

home taking his Bar-Mitzva lessons, or a girl going skating with her "big sister" from Tzivos Hashem. It is the hospital visit to a sick child, or the mail from well-wishers who may have read about him in the Newsletter.

In the Brighton Little League, a Russian boy is playing third base for the Tzivos Hashem "We Keep Shabbos" team. Last year, the same child actually went to a camp run by anti-Jewish missionaries.

In New Orleans, a group of seven children teach one another *brachot* (blessings) at a meeting on their back porch on a Sunday afternoon.

In Milwaukee a child receives a letter from London, England, through "Pinny's Pen-Pal Platoon." In Noti, Oregon, a boy excitedly finds his Moshiach Times in the mailbox.

On a special trip to Brooklyn, a little girl from Oak Park, Michigan, shouts into the microphone with all her might—and 5,000 children repeat after her—one of the "12 Torah Passages," as the Rebbe himself looks on.

Behind the Iron Curtain, an undisclosed number of children attend a Purim Rally; the grand prize— a prayerbook with the Tzivos Hashem sticker inside.

When Tzivos Hashem first began, its young members composed a song. The words expressed an age-old yearning that has burned in the hearts of Jews for almost 2,000 years, and that the darkest days of Exile have not been able to extinguish. It is the now-famous motto which the children themselves created: "We Want Moshiach Now!"

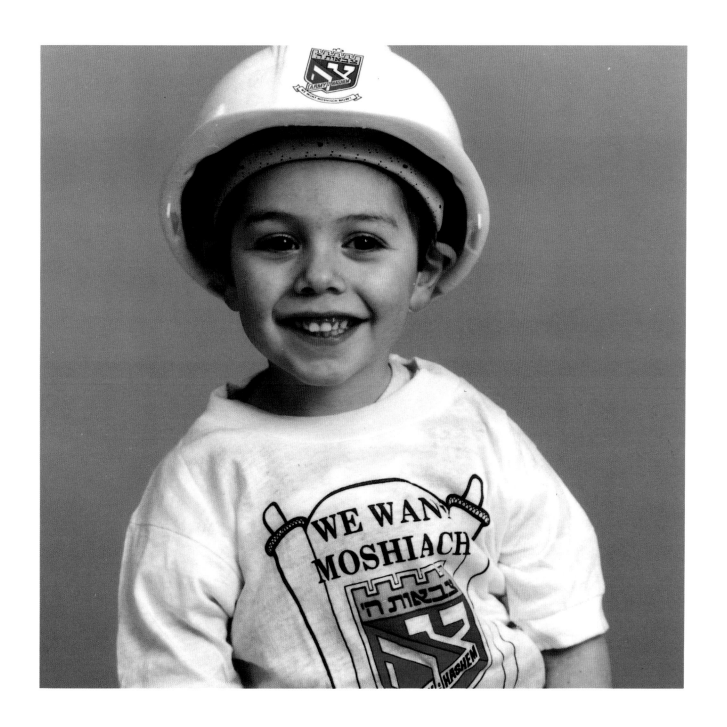

"In the winter of 1988, the "Jewish Children's Expo" at the Jacob Javits Convention Center in Manhattan drew 89,000 children to a kaleidoscope of Jewish history and tradition."

The Young

חנך לנער על פי דרכו גם כי
יזקין לא יסור ממנה
(משלי כב, ו)

*Train a child in
the way he should go;
even when he grows
old he will not depart
from it.
(Proverbs 22:6)*

...Just as wearing *tefillin* every day is a mitzva commanded by the Torah to every individual, whether a great Torah-scholar or a simple person, so too is it an absolute duty for every person to spend a half hour every day thinking about the Torah-education of children, and to do everything in his power—and beyond his power—to inspire children to follow the path along which they are being guided.

Hayom Yom; Tevet 22.

Lag B'Omer Parades: "Everyone loves a parade." On Lag B'Omer huge crowds of children are brought together from schools all over New York. The Rebbe himself attends, speaking to the children, inspiring them to live Jewishly, proudly. In five continents, this example began to be followed, and today Lag B'Omer Parades involve hundreds of thousands of children.

The "Chabad House Room": In 1987, the Rebbe issued a "doubly-urgent suggestion and request to all Jewish children to make their own rooms—the bed, table, etc.—into a "House" of Torah, *tefilla* (prayer) and *gemilut chassadim* (good deeds, charity); to study Torah daily in that room, to offer a prayer to G-d there, to give charity there, into a charity-box (except on Shabbat and *yomtov*)...and that every child should have his or her own *siddur,* his or her own *chumash* (or other Torah-book) and his or her own *pushkeh;* and to inscribe on the flyleaf of these books (also, if possible, on the *pushkeh*), "The world and all it contains belongs to G-d," and the child's name.

From Alaska to Vienna, from Jerusalem to Johannesburg, boys and girls have transformed their rooms by the hundreds of thousands, into "miniature versions" of the *Beit Hamikdash* (Jerusalem's Holy Temple), and into "mini-Chabad Houses."

Main Photo:
Reciting the sh'ma
prayer, declaring G-d's
unity.

A.

B.

C.

D.

E.

F.

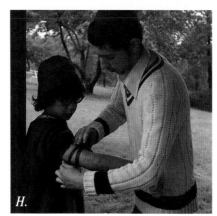

H.

I.

A. Rabbinical College of America; Morristown, New Jersey; the new campus. **B.** Children's Matzo bakery. **C.** Garden view of "The White House" building of the Lubavitch Yeshiva, Melbourne, Australia. **D.** "Torah on the line": Stories for children, a moment of study, or a half-hour in-depth lesson, all are a mere phone-call away. **E.** Camp Gan Israel; Kansas City, Missouri. **F.** Camp Gan Israel; Fenton, Michigan, U.S.A. **G.** Camp Gan Israel, Johannesburg, South Africa. Trip to a gold mine. **H.** Instructing a bar-mitzva-age child in wearing tefillin. Camp Gan Israel, Parksville, New York State, U.S.A. **I.** Campers on a boat trip in Holland.

Main Photo:
Some of the younger
girls at the Beth
Rivkah School in
Melbourne, Australia.
Inset, below:
Shofar factory
demonstration.

The Campaigns For Mitzvot And Holiday Observance

מצות ה׳ ברה מאירת עינים

(תהילים יט, ט)

G-d's mitzva is pure, enlightening the eyes. (Psalms 19:9)

The Jewish Pride Revolution

Our vocabulary has changed.

In the Jewish community today, *"mitzva"* is a common word; *tefillin* are not strange, exotic paraphernalia for the Bar-mitzva boy—but familiar articles; Shabbat candles are no longer "something grandmother lit" on Friday nights—but a commonly observed practice throughout Jewish society; leafy-roofed *sukot* huts?—even "yuppie" suburbanites build them, and *everyone* knows about them. It wasn't always this way.

Just a few short decades ago mitzvot and holidays were the private, quiet domain of the few.

Then came the Rebbe's "mitzva campaigns," and Lubavitch literally took to the streets. "Did you put on *tefillin* today?" "Can I offer you Shabbat candles?" "Can I interest you in some classes on Judaism?" On Wall Street in New York, in London's Picadilly Circus, and in Tel Aviv's Dizengoff Square, Jewish pride and Jewish precepts came out of the closet forever.

The effect? One word sums it up. *Revolution.* An ever-burgeoning renaissance of belief and resurgence of interest in the traditions of Judaism. For countless individuals and families, that mitzva-in-the-street was the first step on the road to an intensified identification with Jewishness, with Jewish education and Jewish observance.

Tefillin: It is the familiar human condition: Heart and mind struggle. Where mind is ineffectual, where emotion dominates unrestricted, the seeds of tragedy are sown. The head-*tefillin* are placed on the head, the seat of intellect, and the hand-*tefillin* on the left arm, opposite the heart. The idea is *subservience of mind and heart* to G-d, and control of the hand and arm—the instruments of *action* of the mind and heart.

47

Main Photo:
Milan, Italy. Chabad
menora in the center
of town.
Inset, below:
The Lubavitch menora
lights up the Paris
skyline on Chanuka.

A. 7 million signed-up: *"A Sefer Torah, a Safer World." In a fragmented world, the call has gone out for every Jewish adult and child to "acquire a letter" in the writing of a collective Sefer Torah in order to be truly united as "The People of the Book." To date, over seven million Jews worldwide, have united through the letters they have acquired. The Hon. Yitzchak Navon, then President of Israel, acquires a letter for his grandson.*
B. *Radio programs internationally promote mitzvot observance.*

מים קרים

C. Kashering a home;
Tel-Aviv, Israel.
*D. A young "soldier"
of Tzivos Hashem
explains the laws of
Passover to a resident
of a senior-citizen
home, who holds
the hand-processed
sh'mura matzo he has
just received from
the child.*

50

In addition, the wearing of *tefillin,* our Sages teach, instills fear in the hearts of our people's enemies. Shortly before the outbreak of the Six-Day-War in June, 1967, the Rebbe launched his unprecedented *tefillin* campaign, whose most famous "outpost" is at the Western Wall, the *Kotel,* in Jerusalem, where several *million* visitors have since observed this cardinal mitzva.

Mezuza: Daily, Jews recite the scriptural command about *mezuza,* in the *sh'ma* prayer: *And you shall write them upon the doorposts of your house, and upon your gates.* The Code of Torah-Law states: *A human king sits inside and his servants guard him from the outside, but you sleep on your beds and the Holy One Blessed-Be-He guards you* (i.e. through the *mezuza* on your doorposts) *from the outside.* In 1974, the Rebbe launched a global *mezuza* campaign, which sparked a total renaissance in *mezuza-*observance worldwide, and, since then, tens of thousands of faded, unfit *mezuzot* have been discovered and replaced and *several hundred thousand* new *mezuzot* have been affixed in Jewish homes.

Kashrut: It was summer, 1975. Speaking in Lubavitch headquarters, with simultaneous telephone transmission to audiences around the globe, the Rebbe addressed the problems caused by lack of *kashrut* observance. He called upon the Jewish family to return to the scrupulous observance of "the kosher laws," addressing his remarks primarily to the woman, who is the dominant influencing factor in keeping a kosher home and who therefore bears the main responsibility for implementing this vital mitzva.

As for the cost factor in changing a kosher kitchen, the Rebbe instructed that a fifty-percent rebate of expenses be made a universal offer. Chabad emissaries began to actively promote the campaign, and today there are untold tens of thousands of homes that have become kosher all around the world.

"On Wall Street in New York, in London's Picadilly Circus, and in Tel Aviv's Dizengoff Square, Jewish pride and Jewish precepts came out of the closet forever."

The Woman In Lubavitch

פי׳ פתחה בחכמה ותורת
חסד על לשונה
(משלי לא, כו)

*She opens her
mouth with wisdom;
the law of kindness
is on her tongue.
(Proverbs 31:26)*

Within the chassidic community, Torah-education has always been considered a vital element in the growth of a young woman. Chabad history is replete with anecdotes of the woman scholar participating with her husband or father in discussions of *halacha* or chassidic philosophy. Such education was given discreetly, quietly, for in that era formal, organized Torah-education for girls did not exist in Jewish society. (This was, of course, neither unusual nor "backward." The concept of formal women's education was also unknown in *general* society at the time— three centuries ago, in Eastern Europe.)

Later, the "revolutionary" idea of formal schooling for girls was cautiously and gingerly introduced into Torah-society in the 1930s, not without some opposition. In Lubavitch, however, the concept was enthusiastically welcomed and supported by the Previous Rebbe. Then, in 1941, the Rebbe arrived in the United States, at which point the "Central Organization for Jewish Education" *(Merkos L'Inyonei Chinuch)* came into being. The Rebbe was appointed its head by his father-in-law (the Previous Rebbe) and one of the first institutions to be established by *Merkos* was the Beth Rivkah Girls' School.

As the challenges and demands of the world beyond the home grew, Chabad-Lubavitch responded by making formal, intensive Torah-education for women an integral part of Jewish life. Today, eloquent testimony to the Rebbe's outlook on women's education is provided by the extensive network of Beth Rivkah and Beth Chana Girls' schools that span the globe from Melbourne, Australia, to the huge campus in Kfar Chabad II in Israel. The level of scholarship in these institutions is unmatched, both in scope as well as depth. Beginning from the earliest ages, through the High School and Seminary level, the schools provide a quality education that equips

The Shabbat and Yomtov candle-lighting campaign, begun in 1974, and developed and maintained by the N'shei Chabad women's organization, has inspired hundreds of thousands of women to begin lighting Shabbat candles. A little girl comes home from kindergarten and asks her mother to let her light Shabbat candles. The following Shabbat the mother joins her daughter; a few weeks later the father joins in with the kiddush, at what has now become an authentic Shabbat table. In several months the entire home has been transformed... It has happened in thousands of homes.

their graduates with the ability to meet any challenge.

For the woman whose Jewish involvement came later in life, Chabad pioneered the concept that Torah-knowledge must be an accessible necessity, not an unreachable luxury. Machon Chana in Brooklyn, New York, Beth Chana in Minneapolis, Minnesota, Machon Alta in Safed, Israel, and Ohel Chana in Australia are notable examples of institutions that have provided an intense intellectual experience to thousands of women, who had little or no background.

Such is the picture in women's education. And what of communal activism?

Shortly after ascending to the leadership of Lubavitch, the Rebbe founded *Agudas N'Shei Chabad* ("Lubavitch Women's Organization"), which was—and remains—unique. It was the first major women's organization which did not emphasize the objectives of fund-raising and auxiliary activities, but *education*. Education of self and of others. *For oneself:* Continuing intellectual and emotional growth through Torah-study, particularly chassidic teachings—which provide the philosophical background for the way of life and pride of the Jewish woman, explaining the uniqueness of her role as *akeret habayit,* "foundation of the home," and the unique powers granted her. *For others:* Dynamic outreach programs, bringing the depth of Torah and the beauty of mitzvot to the attention of the less-informed, particularly to other women and girls, as exemplified by N'shei's leadership of the world-wide Lubavitch campaigns for "Family Purity," Shabbat candle-lighting, *kashrut,* etc.

Today, N'shei seminars and learning programs, speakers bureaus and resource centers are just a few of its activities. In hundreds of communities around the globe N'shei Chabad sponsors the "Week of the Jewish Woman." Annually in Europe and Israel, and biannually in America,

"...eloquent testimony to the Rebbe's outlook on women's education is provided by the extensive network of Beth Rivkah and Beth Chana Girls' schools that span the globe from Melbourne, Australia, to the huge campus in Kfar Chabad II in Israel."

Inset, below: Teaching the alef-bet, teaching Judaism; "my mother my teacher."

thousands of women from all walks of life come together at N'shei Chabad conventions to teach and to learn, to inspire and to be inspired, setting the agenda for the year ahead;

and the girls' division, called *B'nos Chabad,* parallels all these activities on a younger age-level.

The Sh'lucha: The ingredients: An intense Torah-education to the highest levels.

Involvement in communal activism and in outreach endeavors from the earliest years. A co-equal sense of mission constantly re-emphasized by the Rebbe, by teachers and parents.

The result: Women who are uniquely capable of formulating and implementing the programs that can satisfy the challenges and respond to the questions of the times. Thousands of talented women, alongside their husbands, have become emissaries *(sh'luchot)* to various communities.

The first challenge these couples face is to transplant the familiar chassidic environment in an atmosphere of foreign and opposing values; to create the warmth and strength of a chassidic home without the support of a nurturing community, far from family and friends. Quite often the challenge includes the need to learn a new language, to cope with incredible difficulty in obtaining kosher food, and to adjust to a new and strange style of day-to-day living. Many *sh'luchot* are admired for the grace and aplomb with which they rise to these challenges. The generous hospitality which characterizes Lubavitcher homes throughout the world is an expression of the warmth and wisdom of these women.

The *sh'lucha* has the multifaceted role of mother and teacher of her own children, and "mother"/teacher to hundreds of others; a role model to her family and an inspiration to the community as a whole. Typically, she works tirelessly from early morning—directing a school or teaching a class, counselling a parent or planning a program—to the wee hours of the night,

"Annually in Europe and Israel, and biannually in America, thousands of women from all walks of life come together at N'shei Chabad conventions to teach and to learn, to inspire and to be inspired, setting the agenda for the year ahead."

Inset, below: Leading a children's rally.

in addition to her obligations at home. (A number of Lubavitch day-schools and summer camps are administered, directed and managed entirely by women.) The *sh'lucha* embodies the very opposite of the stereotypical notion that leadership must be expressed through public posturing and exposure; she restores the classic Jewish model of leadership through the quiet, unassuming feminine approach of moral authority, influence and personal example.

Every activity and institution depicted throughout this entire book is the accomplishment of a team of emissaries, comprised of both husband and wife.

"...in her role as mother, she is the first to light up the young little souls of the infants, until they begin to shine on their own."

A Letter from the Rebbe: Being a "lamplighter" of Jewish souls is even more emphatically relevant to the Jewish woman, for she is the *actual* candle-lighter, who was given the special divine assignment, extraordinary privilege, and bright mitzva of lighting the candles for the holy Shabbat and festivals; and in a deeper spiritual sense...in her role as "foundation of the home" it is her privilege to light up the Jewish home and everyone in it—including her husband and children, and the friends and visitors who come into the home; and in her role as mother, she is the first to light up the young little souls of the infants, until they begin to shine on their own. Thus she has a very important share in making her house—and the House of Israel as a whole—a fitting home for G-d's Presence, in accordance with G-d's design and desire— *"that I may dwell among (and within) them."*

Adapted from a letter to the Lubavitch Women's Organization Convention, 1980.

Main Photo:
The Rebbe addresses the annual International Convention of N'shei Chabad (Lubavitch Women's Organization), at Lubavitch World Headquarters.

Family Purity

"Family Purity" is the popular translation of *taharat hamishpacha,* the laws regarding such matters as marital relationships and the required periodic immersion in a *mikva*—a "pool" constructed in accordance with certain exacting specifications of Jewish law.

Cardinal. Pivotal. Critical. Essential. All describe the pre-eminent importance in Jewish life of the observance of *taharat hamishpacha.* It enhances the relationship between husband and wife, strengthening the marriage-bonds and fortifying emotional stability. Furthermore, it creates favorable circumstances for parents to bring into the world a child whose body and soul are endowed with a high level of sanctity, for the conduct of mother and father prior to conception affects the refinement-quality of their child, and the kind of desires and drives he or she will have.

Woman to Woman; Mikva Outreach: Chabad women have been at the forefront of the resurgence and renaissance of *mikva'ot* in communities, large and small, throughout the globe, insisting that *mikva'ot* be aesthetically beautiful, even luxurious, implementing educational programs that give participants an understanding of the relevance and vitality of the observance, spending hours with individuals to give the one-to-one contact that is so vitally necessary. They have restored *mikva* and the sanctity of marital life to their rightful roles as the basis of our people's existence.

The Remote Communities Mikva Campaign: Chabad emissaries have always been in the forefront of promoting, teaching and encouraging the observance of *taharat hamishpacha.* In particular, Lubavitch has been the leader in building and repairing *mikva'ot* in communities around the globe— from those hidden in Stalinist Russian cellars, to ultra-modern facilities in the U.S.A., Canada, Israel and the west.

In recent years, a new campaign was launched—to establish *mikva'ot* specifically in small remote towns, far from major Jewish population centers, in communities of 1,000 Jewish families or less. The drive met with an outstanding degree of success which no-one could have predicted, and *mikva* availability has become a reality for several hundred minuscule communities in remote regions. Many towns had never had a *mikva;* others had been devoid of the facility for *decades,* and couples wishing to observe the laws of *mikva* had been compelled to drive (in some cases—to fly) for hours, to the nearest *mikva.*

In North America *mikva'ot* have been built in communities with as few Jewish families as Grand Rapids (Michigan), Columbia (South Carolina), Newport News (Virginia), Muncton and Chomedey in Canada's Quebec Province, and one is nearing completion in Honolulu (Hawaii).

In South America, *mikva'ot* have been established in small Brazilian Jewish communities such as Belem, Belo Horizonte, Curitiba, Porto Allegre, and Recife as well as in Bogota and Cali in Colombia.

Some European and North African remote-location Chabad *mikva'ot* include Montpelier, Noisy, Cannes and Lille in France, Utrecht (Holland), the island of Djerba off the coast of Tunisia, Nabul (Tunisia), and Marrakech and Tangier in Morocco. And in the far reaches of Australia and Asia, there are *mikva'ot* even in Hobart (Tasmania), Brisbane (Queensland) and Hong Kong.

"Cardinal. Pivotal. Critical. Essential. All describe the pre-eminent importance in Jewish life of the observance of taharat hamishpacha."

Inset, below:
The Chabad mikva in Lomita, California, U.S.A.

60

The Forgotten

גם אלה תשכחנה ואנכי לא
אשכחך
(ישעי' מט, טו)

*...but I will not
forget you.
(Isaiah 49:15)*

"He who saves one Jewish life is considered as if he had saved an entire world." This concept imbues *ahavat yisrael* (love of one's fellow) with an urgency, a vitality. To the *shaliach,* each human being is an infinity, the spark is there, and nothing in the entire world is more important. Perhaps most revealing of this outlook is the response to those whose cries are the faintest, the constituencies without advocates—the elderly, the sick, the vulnerable, the imprisoned, the addict, the remote communities. In a word, *the forgotten.*

Small Communities: The small, isolated communities, without access to Jewish resources— these are a major concern. Initial contact is often made through the Student Visitation Programs. Rabbinical students voluntarily give up their personal vacations to travel from place to place, meeting, giving classes, disseminating Jewish publications…planting seeds of Judaism.

The Homeless: In today's modern society, with its highly developed social conscience, one would be justified in believing that all the needs of the Jewish people throughout the world are taken care of. Sadly, this is not always true.

Chabad-Lubavitch worldwide is organized to reach out and help the hungry and the homeless among us. For it has always been the Chabad tradition never to turn away a person in need. Outstanding in the field of social service and rehabilitation is the Chabad House of Westwood, Los Angeles. Here destitute or homeless people can find food, shelter and counselling without question or qualification, in the spacious California facility, at which over a thousand individuals have been accommodated under a 60-day rehabilitation program. Two-thirds of them left with either a job or a place to live, or both, and tens of thousands of meals and units of shelter have been provided.

A. The helping hand of Lubavitch reaches even as far as Tahiti.
B. Rabbis Raskin and Matusof with a group of young campers are warmly received at the palace of Morocco's Prime Minister.
C. The sh'luchim bring a message of encouragement to the old synagogue in Bombay, India and its members.
D. Chabad globe trotting emissaries visiting a Jewish family in New Caledonia—a French island in the Pacific Ocean.

The Vulnerable: The missionaries and cults have found many of our young people vulnerable targets. The response is vigorous and forceful, filling the void with a knowledgeable pride in our heritage. Throughout the world, it is to Lubavitch that distraught parents turn for help in bringing their children home.

The Addict:

Chabad National Drug Abuse Treatment Programs: Once upon a time, Jewish men and women did not get addicted to drugs. Or if one did, certainly no one talked about it.

Times have changed.

Over the course of the last decade the upward spiral of drug use and abuse has taken root and begun to spread in the Jewish community. Each year more and more men and women within the Jewish community identify themselves as drug dependent, and seek treatment.

But for those that desire professional, clinical care in a Jewish environment, there is but one place to turn—the Chabad National Drug Abuse Treatment Programs, operated under the auspices of west coast Chabad-Lubavitch.

The Chabad Men's Residential Rehabilitation Program in Los Angeles, now entering its second decade, is renowned for its success rate—approximately 50%, three times the national average. Recently, the National Women's Rehabilitation Program opened its doors to drug addicted Jewish women. It is the nation's first and only treatment center providing a warm, comfortable Jewish environment for drug dependent women, rich in Jewish cultural milieu, including celebration of Jewish holidays and other traditional observances, and staffed by professionally trained mental health practitioners.

Some remote communities where Chabad-Lubavitch has a permanent presence:
Asuncion, Paraguay;
Hong Kong;
Hobart, Tazmania;
Lima, Peru;
Tunis, Tunisia;
Casablanca, Morocco;
Sandton, South Africa;
Santiago, Chile;
Recife, Brazil;
Tucuman, Argentina.

Some tiny, remote communities, visited regularly by Chabad:
Kobe, Japan;
Calcutta, India;
Kabul, Afghanistan;
Nairobi, Kenya;
Ibidjan, Ivory Coast;
Kinshasa, Zaire;
Quito, Ecuador;
Tahiti;
New Caledonia;
Djerba, Tunisia.

Main Photo:
Chabad counsellor
calms the fears of
a homeless person on
his arrival to the
homeless program of
Lubavitch in Los
Angeles, California.
Inset, below:
Young campers in
Camp Gan Israel of
India write a letter
of appreciation to the
Rebbe.

A unique aspect of the women's program is its ability to house and care for infants and pre-school-age children of addicted mothers during their rehabilitation.

Project Pride. Prevention **R**esources: Information and **D**rug **E**ducation.

An ounce of prevention...

Recent research has identified prevention-education—reaching an individual before experimentation—as the single most promising tactic in the ongoing battle against drug abuse. So it was with an eye to the future that Project PRIDE, Chabad's innovative national network of clinically-based drug prevention and education centers was launched in 1987. The network has grown to include 28 cities strategically located across the United States.

While the majority of the materials at each PRIDE center are suitable for the community-at-large, Chabad has designed a special component aimed specifically at the problem of drug abuse within the Jewish community, who can now turn to a warm, familiar resource for information about drugs. More than 50,000 people—from 6 year olds to senior citizens—are currently being served by this outreach program.

The Prisoner: Finally, those most isolated and forgotten of all—the prisoners. In State and Federal penitentiaries, in prisons in countries throughout the world, Jewish inmates know that Chabad remembers them—and cares, and helps. The Alef Institute, headquartered in Miami, Florida, coordinates visitation, religious services and publication for Jewish prisoners throughout the U.S. Walking through the rain for miles to conduct a *Seder* in a jail, taking hours out of a busy day just to talk to a despairing prisoner, bringing a message of hope and dignity.

Inset, below: The shining, happy face of a child visiting patients in a hospital, on the Purim holiday, bringing mishlo'ach manot food gifts, holiday cheer, and a joyous spirit.

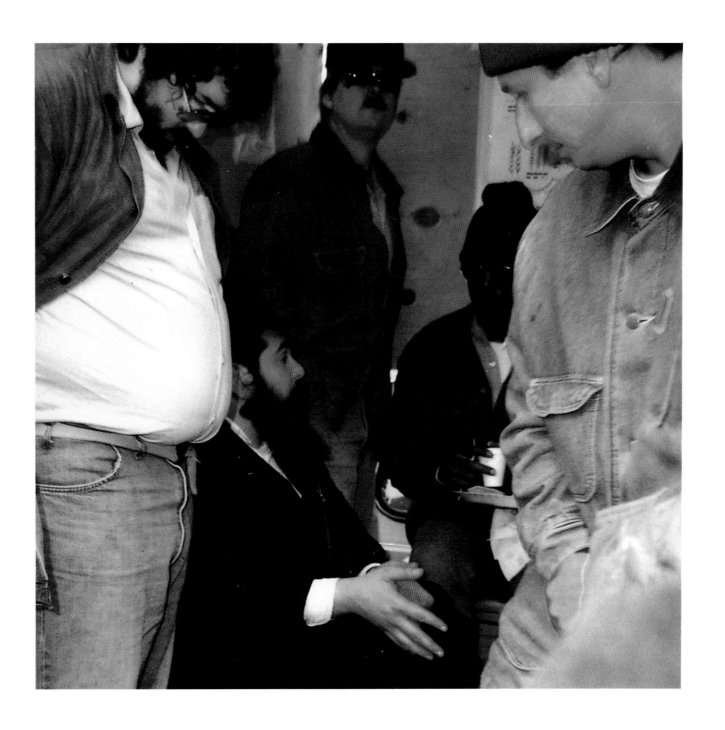

Main Photo:
*Rabbi Moshe Wilhelm
(Portland, Oregon),
brings a message of
hope and encourage-
ment to prisoners
in Portland State
Penitentiary.*
Inset, below:
*A "Chabadnik"
in Israel leaves the
warmth of his home
and family on the
holiday—to bring
Chanuka joy to sol-
diers in underground
bunkers near the Suez
Canal in 1965.*

Soviet Jewry

הנני מביא אותם מארץ צפון
וקבצתים מירכתי ארץ
(ירמי' ל"א. ז)

*I will bring
them forth from the
north country...
(Jeremiah 31:7)*

Russia—the cradle of Chabad. Here Chabad was planted and nurtured; blossomed, flourished and struck its deepest roots. From Liozna and Liadi, from Lubavitch to the furthest reaches of the Pale of Jewish Settlement, Chabad was renowned, revered and cherished.

The Early Years: By the early years of this century, Lubavitch emissaries had reached the furthest corners of the Czarist empire. Sent by Rabbi Sholom Dovber (known as the *Rebbe Rashab,* 1860-1920, fifth leader of Chabad), they visited and inspired Jews in even the remotest communities. The unlearned descendants of the "Cantonists"—Jewish children torn from their families to spend their lives as soldiers of the Czar, oriental Jews in Bukhara, the mountain Jews of Georgia and Daghestan, all welcomed Chabad emissaries sent to teach them Torah and raise their standards of Jewish practice.

The First World War plunged Eastern European Jewish communities into chaos, uprooting large populations and disrupting the traditional Torah education system. Then came the 1917 Bolshevik Revolution.

The Revolution and the Stalin Era: The Revolution opened a frightening new era. Religious education of the young was banned, practice of Judaism was systematically obliterated, and observant Jews—particularly chassidim—were persecuted, arrested, exiled, tortured and shot. To circumcise a child required enormous courage; observing Shabbat and *kashrut* became virtually impossible for the Jewish masses—who had been largely Torah-observant before the Revolution.

"Schneersohns Don't Run.." Most Jewish leaders took advantage of any opportunity to leave the country. But the destiny of Chabad was inextricably bound up with Russian Jewry. The Previous Lubavitcher Rebbe, Rabbi Yosef Yitzchak Schneersohn (1880-1950), son of the Rebbe Rashab,

Main Photo:
Dozens of wedding-canopies line the streets in Elizabeth, New Jersey, in preparation for a Chabad-organized multiple wedding of Russian-Jewish immigrant couples who were denied the opportunity of having religious weddings in the Soviet Union.
Inset, below:
A small group of the brides pose before their wedding.

once told a Czarist police officer: "The Schneersohns don't run away!" True to his word, he stepped into the gap as the only Jewish leader to remain active in the Soviet Union.

The Foundation: Throwing himself into the task at hand, the Previous Rebbe proceeded to build a widespread network of underground institutions—through the length and breadth of that vast land. *Any vestiges of Jewish religious life in the Soviet Union today trace back directly to those foundations.* Although eventually he was forced to leave the country after his harrowing imprisonment and commuted death-sentence in 1927, his shining example of utter self-sacrifice inspired his thousands of chassidim to continue, underground, the work the Rebbe had started—with incredible heroism. Hundreds were shot, thousands were sent to the gulags, but new volunteers always sprang forward to take their places.

The New Chassidim: By the 1930s, older Chassidim could hardly believe their eyes.

"...Oriental Jews in Bukhara, the mountain Jews of Georgia and Daghestan, all welcomed Chabad emissaries sent to teach them Torah and raise their standards of Jewish practice."

Traditionally a Chassid had been one who had met the Rebbe and developed a strong personal attachment to him, continuing to visit him regularly for renewed inspiration. But here was a generation of youngsters educated in the cellars and attics of the underground, on the run from city to city to escape arrest, often without teachers and mentors. Few of these boys had ever seen the Rebbe. Yet they yearned with every fiber of their young souls for their Rebbe, and were utterly devoted to what he held dearest.

Amidst the ruins of the once proud Russian Jewry arose a generation that stood ready to offer their very lives in the struggle to preserve Judaism.

The Inner Spark: Unfortunately, the pall and fear hanging over Stalin's Russia prevented this from becoming the experience of most Jewish youth. Sheer force of circumstances, later perpetuated

*Main Photo:
Moscow, 1987. Jewish
youngsters un-
ashamedly pore over
Jewish books on
display by Chabad's
Kehot Publication
Society at the Moscow
Book Exhibit.*

by simple ignorance, estranged the Jewish masses from their faith. But the inner Jewish spark could never be extinguished. Most Soviet Jews retained awareness of their Jewish identity, usually without even grasping what "being Jewish" really meant.

The Return: Recent years dramatically illustrate the eternal validity of that rationally inexplicable phenomenon—the miracle of Jewish survival despite all efforts to destroy it in body and spirit. How does one explain that Jews assimilated for four generations can now, over 70 years after the Revolution, suddenly be awakened to the true meaning of their Jewishness and valiantly begin to observe *mitzvot*—despite continuing incredible hardships? How do we account for scientists and intellectuals, reared on Marxist-Leninist dogma, who repudiate atheistic materialism and grope their way back to their ancestral roots? How can we comprehend a movement of return to Judaism throughout the length and breadth of the U.S.S.R., sparked by Lubavitch?

Let My People Know: Some of the early Russian emigres had experienced a certain sense of disappointment with their reception in their new domicile, a neglect of their spiritual needs. But Lubavitch was there to fill the gap, to make the transition from "Let my people go" to "Let my people know." The Rebbe, in the early 1970s, issued a call for intensified assistance to those who had already left Russia. The response was immediate: Lubavitch programs were established wherever Soviet Jews arrived, to help them both materially and spiritually; particularly large-scale programs and institutions were founded in Los Angeles, Toronto, New York and Jerusalem. "F.R.E.E." (Friends of Refugees from Eastern Europe) was founded in New York in the late 1960s, with branches and similar programs initiated by Lubavitch offices in most North American cities, and several foreign lands, through the 1970s and 1980s.

Inset below: Professor Herman Branover. Dr. Branover is a Lubavitch baal teshuva ("returnee" to Jewish practice) from the Soviet Union who heads the renowned Shamir organization and coordinates outreach programs to the constantly-arriving Russian immigrants to Israel. A professor of Physics at Ben Gurion University of the Negev in Beersheba, Branover is the world expert in Magneto-hydrodynamics.

The prestigious "Shamir" organization—concentrating on helping scientists and intellectuals—was founded in Israel.

First Hand Experience: The great success of these groups is primarily due to the fact that their founders and workers are themselves Soviet emigres, the second and third generation of Chabad activists produced by the underground Russian *yeshivot*. They speak the same language, and are acquainted with the background and problems of the Soviet Jew from first-hand experience; the Soviet emigres are their own brothers, their companions in suffering. In fact, these Lubavitch activists did the same work back in the Soviet Union—with the difference that there it was in a cellar, while now they work openly, in the streets of Manhattan or Hollywood.

A Vast New Project: When Soviet Jewish emigration increased in the late 1960s and early 1970s, the Rebbe arranged that new Chabad settlements in Israel be founded to accommodate them. It is now the 1980s; once again a considerably increased emigration is expected, in response to which the Rebbe has set in motion a vast new project with a revolutionary approach to the much-discussed problem of the emigrants opting to settle in countries other than Israel. As in similar cases, the Rebbe has stressed *the positive,* providing an environment attractive and conducive to Soviet Jewish settlement in every dimension—the religious and spiritual, the cultural and linguistic, the economic and financial. It is the creation of an entire "city within a city," to contain, eventually, its own schools, synagogues, municipal facilities and training centers—all exclusively for Soviet emigrants, to be built in the Holy City of Jerusalem.

Change the Suitcase Label: Word spread fast in the Soviet Union. Within weeks of the June 1987 birth of the Shamir Neighborhood in northern Jerusalem—which will eventually accommodate

"...these Lubavitch activists did the same work back in the Soviet Union—with the difference that there it was in a cellar, while now they work openly, in the streets of Manhattan or Hollywood."

hundreds of families, with special arrangements for academic, professional and technolog-

ical job-opportunities nearby—Soviet Jews were already changing the labels on their suitcases from

"New York" to "Jerusalem."

Hi-Tech Jobs: The Shamir Center for Advanced Technologies is a commercial enterprise

that will supply the first seventy high-level jobs. Its first three departments—Computers, Physics,

and Chemistry—are involved in high-tech projects, serving both Israeli and overseas

industries. At the same time, Shamir runs a high-level Torah Study Institute for the newly arrived

immigrants, where they can spend part of their day making up for lost time in study of their

ancestral heritage.

Chabad and Russian Jewry: This ambitious project epitomizes the work of Chabad-Lubavitch

for Jews of Russia—devotion to helping them materially as well as spiritually. It is part of a process

that began over two centuries ago in Russia and continues today, seventy years after

a frightful revolution.

For Soviet Jewry and Chabad-Lubavitch are inextricably bound together.

"Within weeks of the June 1987 birth of the Shamir Neighborhood in northern Jerusalem...Soviet Jews were already changing the labels on their suitcases from "New York" to "Jerusalem."

Inset, below: A team of doctors and Lubavitch activists congratulate a 13-year-old Russian-Jewish immigrant after his brit mila—the covenant he could not enter behind the Iron Curtain.

A. Shamir village, Jerusalem. Residential complex for Russian immigrants. Sponsored by U.S. industrialist Ronald O. Perelman.
B. "Satec"— Shamir Center for Advanced Technologies.
C. Joseph Gutnick, Australian entrepeneur and financier—and benefactor of Satec—addressing a reception in honor of the Shamir/Satec ground-breaking in Jerusalem, at the "Beit Hanassi" (house of Israel's president). From left to right: Joseph Gutnick, Professor. Herman Branover, Hon. Yakov Tzur (Israel's Minister of Absorption), President Herzog, General Arik Sharon, Hon. Teddy Kollek (Mayor of Jerusalem).

The Beauty Of The Elderly

והדרת פני זקן
(ויקרא יט, לב)

Give respect to the old.
(Leviticus 19:32)

Some years ago, it happened that an American college student was vacationing in Israel, and paid a visit to some distant relatives he had never met before. His hosts, a large family of recent immigrants from Eastern Europe, spoke very little English, and lived a deeply religious traditional lifestyle. It was the young man's first exposure to Judaism of any kind. Nothing in his previous experience had prepared him for what he termed the "culture shock" of seeing a way of life so vastly different from his own. Later, when asked what it was that impressed him the most, he replied, "It was the old people, the grandparents and great-grandparents." He had never before seen elderly people who were so deeply respected by their children, and children's children, who continued to lead such productive lives, and who remained so cheerful and filled with inner peace.

What a contrast to the depression and feelings of uselessness that afflict so many senior citizens in our society today! The popular view of old people is that they are incompetent, "over the hill." Age is considered a serious handicap; the aged are made to feel that they are a burden to those around them. In the business world, they are often forced to retire and make way for younger men, or given some minor niche in the company hierarchy—"kicked upstairs," where their advice can be conveniently ignored.

Within the family, they are often placed in nursing homes and remembered on Father's Day, Mother's Day, and occasional Sunday afternoons. And the resultant psychological and physical debilitation serves only to reinforce their second-class status in the eyes of the young.

Most unfortunate is the fact that society thereby turns its back on the tremendous stock of hard-earned experience and wisdom which older people possess. They have been through various trials and tribulations, have learned ways of coping with many of life's toughest problems,

*Main Photo:
The elderly—
an invaluable resource
of sage counsel to
younger people. Rabbi
Mendel Futerfass,
renowned chassidic
elder, conducting
a joyous farbrengen
(festive gathering
in the chassidic spirit).*

and can be an invaluable resource of sage counsel to younger people lacking this experience.

Such a priceless store of knowledge is acquired only over the course of many years. But instead of utilizing this valuable asset to the full, quality is callously cast aside for the doubtful advantage of youth.

In the summer of 1980, the Rebbe delivered a public address on the occasion of the 36th *yahrzeit* of his father, Rabbi Levi Yitzchak Schneerson, who was Chief Rabbi of Yekatarinoslav (now Dnepropetrovsk), U.S.S.R. The Rebbe spoke at length about the plight of the elderly in contemporary society, and called for a vigorous, widespread effort to rectify the situation.

"There should be no such thing as compulsory retirement," he said. "Older people who are compelled, for whatever reason, to relinquish their job or positions, should be helped to redirect their lives productively, for their own sake and for the benefit of the younger generation."

The Rebbe proposed that special Torah-study classes be established in every community, for men, and for women, on a level appropriate to the particular group. Old-age homes, where the staff are constantly seeking new ways of keeping their clientele occupied and happy, are particularly suitable for introducing daily Torah classes. But the Rebbe made clear that he was addressing himself to the needs of *all* the elderly, and that those who do lead active, productive lives should also take part in these programs. He suggested that the groups be named *Kolel Tiferes Z'Keinim* ("Glory of the Elders"), and he expressed his heartfelt appreciation for those who would add the name "Levi Yitzchak," after his father, who had so courageously dedicated his life to the advancement of Torah-study among Jews of all ages. In addition, the name *Bais Chochmas Noshim* (the "Wisdom of Women") was given to classes organized for elderly women.

"Many years bring wisdom," says the Biblical verse (Job 32:7). And the Talmud comments

"Older people who are compelled, for whatever reason, to relinquish their job or positions, should be helped to redirect their lives productively, for their own sake and for the benefit of the younger generation."

Inset, below:
A team of Chabad school children visit a senior citizens home.

that the minds of elderly scholars become more settled with age. The classes, established

through Chabad centers internationally, and named *Kolel Tiferes Z'keinim Levi Yitzchak* have become

a means of making the later years truly "golden years." Older people can once again

become respected members of the community; feelings of inferiority are being replaced with wisdom,

with Torah content; and the elderly are being inspired to share their ever-deepening wisdom

with the younger generations, for the benefit of all. These many thousands of study groups are indeed

bringing blessings to every individual, regardless of age, and to society as a whole—as alluded to

in the Fifth Commandment: "Honor your father and mother, so that your days may be lengthened

(in quality as well as quantity) upon the earth which the L-rd your G-d is giving you."

"...feelings of inferiority are being replaced with wisdom, with Torah content; and the elderly are being inspired to share their ever-deepening wisdom with the younger generations, for the benefit of all."

*Inset, below:
One of the many thousands of Torah-study groups for the elderly organized around the globe by Chabad-Lubavitch.*

Israel

ארץ אשר תמיד עיני ה'
אלקיך בה מרשית השנה ועד
אחרית שנה
(דברים יא, יב)

*The land upon which
the eyes of G-d your
G-d constantly gaze...
(Deuteronomy 11:12)*

Eretz Yisrael. The Holy Land. A land uniquely endeared to the Jewish people and to G-d, as the land "..upon which the eyes of G-d your G-d gaze from the beginning of the year until year's end."

Deuteronomy 11:12.

For hundreds of thousands of Israelis—from the core of the country to the farthest reaches of its borders—month by month, day by day, moment by moment—the work of Chabad profoundly affects the very fabric of daily life in Israel.

In Tel Aviv a Russian immigrant spends sleepless nights in his newly won freedom straining to learn a new language, adjusting to new social customs, making friends, worrying over the loneliness of his young children.

A woman in an impoverished district, her husband long gone to work, her children out of school and on the streets from 12:30 in the afternoon till bedtime, sits in the 95 degree heat of a three-bedroom apartment that houses her family of eight.

On the cool, tiled patio of a villa in Carmiel, a group of professors sip their cocktails, discussing in measured intellectual tones the latest developments in astrophysics research as they await the arrival of the local Chabad rabbi, for their weekly class in chassidic philosophy.

A young soldier, spending his first Chanuka away from family and friends, stands a cold, wet guard along the Lebanese border, his bravery and patriotism struggling to combat the numbness in his feet, the emptiness in his heart.

These are the people of Israel. From every corner of the world. From every imaginable background and descent; of every economic and social status. Of every level of religious observance from the most religious and chassidic, to the most secular and cynical. Chabad has accomplished what

Main Photo:
The study-hall
(Beit Midrash) of the
senior yeshiva in
Kfar Chabad,
a renowned academy
of higher talmudic
studies.

was deemed *impossible*—to have open channels of communication to them all, to be endeared to all and respected by all.

Israel is a country beset with economic struggles, internal factionalism, and a growing materialism that threatens to erode its religious and moral foundations. In the face of this, Chabad provides the hope and idealism so desperately needed for Israel's vitality. Chabad infuses those they touch with joy and pride in the uniqueness of the Jewish people and the holiness of the Land of Israel—so that their life takes on purpose and meaning, transcending the hardships of every day existence. Chabad Houses everywhere hum with a steady flow of people needing help, finding a job, paying a bill, or feeding the family; while others seek religious guidance, a pair of *tefillin,* or help with their son's bar-mitzva.

The Jews of Israel. All loved and served by Chabad in a thousand ways, every day, and with an overflowing heart. Indeed Lubavitch is accepted by hundreds of thousands as the spiritual heart-beat of the country, and everyone knows *"Tzach,"* the Lubavitch Youth Organization—Chabad's general activities arm.

For the Children: Over 300,000 boys and girls in Israeli cities and villages attend informal weekly classes under the auspices of the Tzivos Hashem organization; 40,000 children participate in day-camps during the summer vacation; *Shabbat* afternoon gatherings are conducted weekly in over 300 communities; every year thousands of children gain their first exposure to Judaism by spending a *Shabbat* in the picturesque chassidic community of Kfar Chabad.

In the pre-Purim educational campaign, literally tens of thousands of children actively participate in the *mitzva* of giving gifts of goodies to friends and total strangers; throughout the following month,

"For hundreds of thousands of Israelis—from the core of the country to the farthest reaches of its borders—month by month, day by day, moment by moment— the work of Chabad profoundly affects the very fabric of daily life in Israel."

Inset, below: A delighted Israeli school-child with the hand-processed sh'mura matzo he has just received during his school's visit to the Kfar Chabad matzo bakery.

Main Photo:
Students operating
one of the high-speed
presses at the
school of printing,
one division of the
Schaver/Lazaroff/
Tannenbaum Voca-
tional Training Cam-
pus in Kfar Chabad.

fleets of buses converge on the Kfar Chabad village in order to show schools how handmade

sh'mura matzo is baked (and this means taking home new learning, new songs, a new Passover *Haggada,*

and a sample of real *matzo*). To meet the learning needs of this vast array of young

people, mobile and conventional libraries lend out books and tapes, and a computer center develops

state-of-the-art educational programs.

The Chabad Houses: From Nahariyah in the north to Eilat in the south, 130 Chabad Houses

serve the adults with open minds and warm hearts. They organize teams of volunteers to

check *mezuzot,* conduct study sessions, make kitchens kosher, distribute *Shabbat* candles in hospitals,

visit and teach the elderly, help in the rehabilitation of prisoners, and the list goes on.

The Festivals: Each festival sparks off a range of public service projects—scores of *sukot*

on wheels, public *menora*-lighting and rallies for Chanuka, *megilla*-reading and *shallach-manot*

distribution on Purim, etc. One of the annual activities peculiar to Eretz Yisrael is the

educational program for *Tu BiShevat,* the New Year for Trees, when religious agricultural laws associ-

ated with the Holy Land are highlighted. On Lag Ba'Omer, hundreds of colorful parades,

involving over a quarter of a million children, take place throughout the country.

The Institutions of Education: All of Chabad's educational institutions are qualitatively

remarkable. In addition, some are quantitatively outstanding—in terms of enrollment, success-rate,

scope and beauty of their buildings and grounds, sophistication of their equipment and

front-line educational technology. A few examples: The *yeshiva* called Torat Emet, founded in Hebron

in 1912, and today a major institution of higher Torah-learning in Jerusalem; the great *yeshivot*

of Kfar Chabad, whose academic standards are respected worldwide, and whose senior students often

Main Photo:
A cavalcade of
Chabad-Lubavitch
"mitzva-mobiles"
leaving their base in
Natzeret, Israel, at
dusk, on a Chanuka
mission of joy and
inspiration to various
Israeli army bases
across the country.

volunteer to spend their rare free Shabbat in a *kibbutz* where there is neither a kosher kitchen nor a synagogue; the magnificent campus of the girls' high school and seminary complex of Beit Rivka; the forward-looking vocational schools in Kfar Chabad, offering training in agriculture, carpentry, printing and engineering; the Ascent Institute in Safed, with its English-language outreach seminars and vibrant publications; Machon Alta, with its intellectually stimulating study programs for women of college age; Shifra and Puah, which recruits teams of teenage girls to cheerfully take over the household tasks of women immediately after childbirth. These and many other institutions (not mentioned, for brevity's sake) have made a major impact upon Israeli society.

Nachalat Har Chabad: In 1969, a second major settlement was established by the Rebbe in southern Israel. (Some noticed that the initials of its name, *Nachalat Har Chabad*, were the letters of *Chana,* name of the Rebbe's mother, Rebbetzin Chana, who had passed away in 1964.)

"From Nahariya in the north to Eilat in the south, 130 Chabad Houses serve the adults with open minds and warm hearts."

Like its counterpart Kfar Chabad (founded in 1948), the town has its own schools, *yeshivot,* synagogues and medical centers—as well as textile factories and other industries.

Lubavitchers in the Army: The scene had an aura of surrealism. It was the holiest day of the year, Yom Kippur, in the Lubavitch town of Kfar Chabad, in 1973. In the three major *shuls,* the gentle, yet awe-inspiring, voice of the *chazzan* could be heard over the hum of praying. A sea of white *kittel* robes (worn *only* on this special day), the *tallit* shawls covering the faces. Here and there a quiet sobbing. The Day of Judgement; the day of supreme self-honesty. Shattering the atmosphere—the raucous diesel engines of army transport trucks, raising clouds of dust as they roared down the deserted roads of the town, and came to stop outside the *shul.* Invasion. War. Call-up. Shock. The word spread like lightning throughout the sea of worshippers.

"The widows of all of Israel's fallen heroes are regularly visited by one of a team of dedicated women."

Main Photo:
The Beth Rivkah Girls' School campus in Kfar Chabad, Israel, as seen from the air.
Inset, below:
In the computer training center of the campus.

Pikuach nefesh, danger to life, mandated violation even of Yom Kippur observance.
Chassidim began to file out of *shul* and clamber into the trucks, their *tallit* and *kittel* removed,
but still incongruous in their long black coats.

The Lubavitchers were on the way to their units and their posts as part of Israel's army,
joining the other defenders of their people, "as one man, with one heart." *Exodus 19:2; Rashi.*

Lubavitchers for the Army: The special relationship of Chabad with the Israel Defense Forces
is legendary. "Chabadniks" (the affectionate Israeli colloquialism for Lubavitch chassidim) will tramp
through miles of mud to bring Chanuka or Purim cheer to an isolated, desolate army base.
Cherished by the soldiers of Israel, their selflessness and self-sacrifice is seen as a genuine expression
of love and unity with these brave men who steadfastly guard our Holy Land. These are not
isolated, sporadic visits. Visitation by Chabad takes place on *an army-wide scale* every Sukot, Chanuka
and Purim, and there is a highly-organized program of regular visitation by the "mitzva-tanks,"
which have become famous on the Lebanese front. All of which is in addition to the person-to-person
warmth exuded by the men of Chabad to their buddies, when they serve their tour of duty
in the Armed Forces.

War Orphans and Widows: In 1967, following the Six-Day-War, David Golombowicz, a Chabad soldier,
fell at the Suez Canal. His young widow, Shifra, having just given birth to a baby boy,
felt the crushing loneliness, the devastating emptiness and loss—and resolved to establish an organization to help others like herself. Years of effort began. And today? The widows of all of
Israel's fallen heroes are regularly visited by one of a team of dedicated women. Every Purim a sisterly
volunteer brings *mishloach manot;* every Pesach each bereaved family is brought handmade *matzo;*

*Inset, below:
Students at the
Lubavitch Vocational
School in Kfar
Chabad, Israel, are
not only trained to be
expert computer engi-
neers, but are also
given the opportunity
to further their
religious studies.*

Main Photos:
Upper: The renowned soup-kitchen run by Kolel Chabad for the needy of Jerusalem.
Lower: A drafting class in session at the Kfar Chabad Vocational School for Boys.
Inset, below:
At the Beth Rivkah College in Kfar Chabad, a young woman trains to be a seamstress.

and on Chanuka the friend from Chabad is there again...The ongoing, unsung, year-round support programs are actively encouraged by the Ministry of Defense. And that is just the beginning ...

Year after year, for three weeks every summer, the families of the Lubavitch town of Kfar Chabad open their homes to hundreds of war orphans; children who, along with their mothers and siblings, have been nurtured by Chabad since the tragic death of their fathers.

The children attend summer camps and live with families while their mothers enjoy a well needed respite from the ceaseless strain of raising children without fathers to help, without husbands to love. While they have fun at camp, these children learn the true meaning of *hachnasat orchim,* the mitzva of welcoming guests. In the minds of these children—many from non-religious homes—Judaism becomes associated with a loving family, open arms, a kind word, and a kindred spirit that helps heal the ache of a lost father.

"The Lubavitchers were on the way to their units and their posts as part of Israel's army, joining the other defenders of their people, as one man, with one heart."

And at the annual Chabad bar-mitzva celebration for IDF war orphans, hundreds of these boys gather, surrounded by family and friends, top army generals and government leaders. Each boy receives presents and a special gift from Chabad of *tefillin,* and thousands of well-wishers dance joyously as they enter Jewish manhood.

Publications for the Public: Religiously, Israel is complex; a place where the religious foundations of Judaism are often scorned beneath the proliferation of secular values, and Jewish children can receive little or no traditional Jewish education. In response to this, Chabad has launched a massive campaign of Jewish education to Israel's young. Millions of colorful books, pamphlets, brochures and posters are distributed throughout Israel, urging, instructing, and inspiring Israeli children to the proper observance of holidays and mitzvot.

Kolel Chabad: The leaders of Chabad-Lubavitch were actively involved in settlement

of the Holy Land, as long ago as two hundred years. From 1776 onward, they raised funds throughout

Europe to aid the economically beleaguered inhabitants of Israel. The oldest Jewish charitable

organization in the Holy Land is Kolel Chabad, founded in 1788 by Rabbi Schneur Zalman of Liadi

(1745-1812), first leader of the movement, and continuously active since that time. Kolel Chabad treats

Israel's needy as if they were their own brothers and sisters. At the subsidized supermarkets

run by this unique humanitarian organization, the poor maintain their self-esteem by buying the food,

not taking outright charity. The elderly homeless avail themselves of free daily hot meals

at Kolel Chabad's soup kitchens, while other low-income families receive a variety of social and

humanitarian services, including free heaters installed in their meager apartments,

and assistance with heating bills.

Kolel Chabad provides temporary apartments, food and utensils, and many other services

to newly-arrived Russian immigrants, and sponsors Russian-language literature for these spiritually-

impoverished families. The organization heads a nationwide program of hospital visitation for children,

particularly during the festival seasons. For example, during Chanuka, Kolel Chabad is famous

for turning up in the wards of chronically ill children, with gifts, clowns and hot potato-*latkes*.

The Mobile Centers/"Mitzva Tanks": It is an insurmountable task to attempt to describe

the gargantuan accomplishments of the Chabad Mobile Centers or "tanks" as they have become

known, headquartered in the northern city of Upper Nazareth. Instead, let the figures speak

for themselves: Ten large and seven small mobile centers visit 1,050 settlements from snow-capped

Mount Hermon in the north to lonely *kibbutzim* on the hot, dry shores of the Dead Sea.

"The elderly homeless avail themselves of free daily hot meals at Kolel Chabad's soup kitchens, while other low-income families receive a variety of social and humanitarian services."

Inset, below: Giant Lubavitch childrens' rally at the Western Wall.

In addition, regular visitation programs are maintained to all Army bases and outposts from the border with Lebanon to the frontier with Egypt, and in the Jordan Valley and Golan Heights. Lectures and classes on various levels are given to men, women and children by the Lubavitch instructors staffing the "tanks." Qualified scribes are attached to the units, to examine *tefillin* and *mezuzot,* and supply new ones. During an average week, 400 classes are given to 17,000 soldiers, civilians and children! Sometimes the mobile centers keep moving; sometimes they stay in a village or town for Shabbat. And in the course of a year, approximately one million Israelis study about their heritage through the "tanks."

"Mobile centers visit 1,050 settlements from snow-capped Mount Hermon in the north to lonely kibbutzim on the hot, dry shores of the Dead Sea."

Inset, below: Bringing etrog, lulav, and Sukot joy to a wounded soldier.

Main Photo:
"Chabadnik" soldiers.
The morale of Luba-
vitch fighting-men
in the Israel Defense
Forces—is legendary;
they not only dis-
charge their duties
joyously, they are also
a constant source
of inspiration and
encouragement to their
buddies.

The Happiest Purim Of My Life!

Dear Men of Chabad:

I am not an emotional person, and I certainly don't usually verbalize my feelings.

But I feel a profound need to write you and thank you for your fantastic visit with us, last Purim.

It was cold, rainy and depressing. In our desolate army outpost there was no hint of Purim joy.

Each of us sat in silence, introspective; not too difficult to guess what we were thinking about.

Suddenly, as if from another planet, in bursts a bunch of happy, singing guys. I've got to admit, at first the whole thing seemed so weird, so out of place, that I just laughed at it. But in no time at all you fellows managed to drag me and my buddies into the joy you had generated.

My family was never religious. Sure, we always celebrated Purim—but only with "the fun part"— parties, parades and masquerades; this was the first time in my life that I heard how the Purim *megilla* is read. You gave us bags of Purim goodies, a few little sips of vodka, and you actually managed to get us dancing. We totally forgot the gloomy atmosphere that had pervaded the outpost before you arrived.

That Purim, which I had thought would be the most depressing I had ever spent, was transformed—thanks to you people—to the most joyous and wonderful I have ever experienced. You left us in a state of amazement. I still do not understand where you derive so much strength and joy and self-sacrifice to leave your own homes on the Purim holiday and go out into the rain and the cold to gladden the hearts of some soldiers stuck in a forlorn hole.

But one thing I do know; you are fantastic people!

Gil Reuvaini, Israel Defense Forces

March 16, 1987

Main Photo:
A young Chabad yeshiva-student brings an inspirational message of the victory "of the few over the many" to an Israeli military training camp for officers in the sun-drenched Negev.
Inset, below:
Purim comes to an isolated army-post— courtesy of Chabad!

Chabad
On Campus

במקום שבעלי תשובה
עומדים צדיקים גמורים אינם
יכולים לעמוד שם
(ברכות לד. ב)

*In the place where
penitents stand—not
even the perfectly
righteous can stand
there.
(Berachot 34b.)*

Foresight; the 1950s: The year was 1951. The tidal wave of secularism seemed to be sweeping even the most well-anchored youth away from their moorings. Few imagined that any young Jews would remain faithful to their origins for more than one generation. At 770 Eastern Parkway, Lubavitch World Headquarters in New York, a noted American writer was interviewing the Rebbe— and was amazed when the Rebbe told him, "we must work to reclaim ever-widening circles of non-religious Jews." At that time it seemed utterly outside the realm of possibility.

The Early "Returnees": Not satisfied with words alone, the Rebbe was already then addressing groups of as-yet non-observant college students whom he encouraged his followers to bring to "770." We find letters he wrote to other followers, advising them how to deal with students.

The tempo of student outreach increased, and in 1962, the world's first-ever *yeshiva* for *baalei teshuva* ("returnees" to Judaism) opened its doors in New York.

An Historical "First": In the past, *baalei teshuva* had been few and far between. Some great classic narratives about chassidic leaders of past generations tell how they occasionally reclaimed one or two such Jewish souls long lost to their ancestral heritage. But suddenly, here were hundreds of young people rejecting their generation's secular attitudes and enthusiastically accepting the eternal values of their faith. Here, *for the first time in history,* was an entire *yeshiva* devoted exclusively to *baalei teshuva*.

The Sixties: By now, college youth throughout America and western Europe were openly declaring their disappointment with the materialistic outlook of their peers. They utterly rejected the values taken for granted for decades; they discarded the long-held notion that a professional career, and the "almighty dollar" was the solution to all problems. The age of the Sixties

*Main Photo:
A university Chabad-
House director and
his student friends,
on campus.
Inset, below:
Chabad House at
University of
Michigan, Ann Arbor,
Michigan, U.S.A.*

had dawned, replete with rebellion, protest, hippiedom and the drug-culture.

Channelling the Energy: Many recoiled from the bizarre behavior and language of the students. But the Rebbe diagnosed this seemingly negative outburst of energy as a positive revolt against hypocrisy and materialism: "They have already come half-way by rejecting the wrong values of their generation. Now we must accept their challenge and show them how to come the other half of the journey—back to the values of Torah."

To the Campuses! Students throughout the U.S.A. became accustomed to the sight of young, bearded chassidic rabbis spending time on college campuses. They were "great guys for rap sessions." They actually *welcomed* questions, absolutely loved the tough challenges, and could go on giving solid, intellectual arguments till the wee hours of the morning.

Feeling "at Home": But they didn't stop there. They were also genuinely friendly and hospitable. As discussions drew to a close from sheer fatigue, the Lubavitcher young men would invite students to their homes for a coffee or a hot meal. The students immediately felt at home in the "open-house" atmosphere, felt part of the family with the Chabad rabbi, his wife and their lively, beautiful children. In such an atmosphere it was a pleasure to put on *tefillin*, or to spend Shabbat.

Encounter with Chabad: In 1962 began the "Encounter with Chabad" program of weekends in Crown Heights—the Brooklyn neighborhood housing the central Lubavitch institutions and community. Attended by hundreds of student "seekers," and by many of their professors, the "Encounter" provided an opportunity to appreciate Torah-observant life in a chassidic setting— particularly since the students were housed with a Lubavitcher family and participated in their lifestyle and their Shabbat.

"What Lubavitch has done and continues to do for the Jewish student community on university campuses around the globe, is legendary. The vision has become reality..."

During the weekend, the students also sat in on seminars and lectures by prominent scholars, making it a wonderful blend of the intellectual, emotional and practical. For many, "Encounter" was the first step on their return journey to Torah and mitzvot.

Campus Chabad House: In 1967, the first university "Chabad House" opened its doors on the campus of UCLA in Los Angeles (though the establishment of Lubavitch centers in general began in 1959). As its director presented the key to the Rebbe, he was amazed when the Rebbe told him that this would be the first of many—"like a chain of supermarkets!" Yet these words did not take long to materialize. Today there are hundreds of Chabad Houses for students on or near college campuses around the world; they have saved tens of thousands of our children from inter-marriage and have brought many more back to Jewish commitment.

No Judgment: What endears Chabad rabbis to the students is their downright friendliness, their openness and their non-judgmental approach to every student. And they never give up on any Jew; they seek out even the most distant and most alienated, even those deeply involved in cults or drugs, even those who hardly realize they are Jewish.

Reality and Vision: Today, those who have returned to Judaism via Chabad-on-Campus number in the tens of thousands throughout the world. Some are now themselves Lubavitch emissaries, rabbis or educators. These *baalei teshuva* are fruits of a vision. Despite the much-discussed "vanishing Jew syndrome," despite the ridicule from non-observant (and even some observant) Jews as to the possibility of reclaiming Jewish youth, the Rebbe's vision has been dramatically vindicated. What Lubavitch has done and continues to do for the Jewish student community on university campuses around the globe, is legendary. The vision has become reality...

A student at an Ivy League college looked up from lunch to see a Rabbi in a long black coat standing on a chair. "Today is Rosh Hashana. I know some of you didn't get a chance to hear the shofar. So I'll blow the shofar for you now!" That student wrote later: "There was no judgment, no lecture; just love and concern. At that moment began my return to Judaism..."

A Partial List of Universities Served by Chabad-Lubavitch:

U.S.A. Alabama University of Alabama, Birmingham **Arizona** Arizona State University, Tempe □ University of Arizona, Tulsa **California** University of California at Berkeley, Berkeley □ University of California at Irvine, Irvine □ U.C.L.A., Los Angeles □ National University, National City □ University of California at Santa Barbara, Santa Barbara □ Grosmont University, San Diego □ Palomar University, San Diego □ San Diego State University, San Diego □ University of California at San Diego, San Diego **Colorado** University of Colorado, Boulder □ University of Colorado, Denver **Connecticut** Trinity College, Hartford □ Wesleyan University, Middletown □ University of New Haven, New Haven □ Yale University, New Haven □ University of Connecticut, Storrs □ University of Hartford, W. Hartford **Delaware** University of Delaware, Newark **Florida** F.I.U., Miami Beach □ University of Miami, Miami Beach □ Nova University, North Miami Beach □ University of Central Florida, Orlando, Florida □ University of Southern Florida-Tampa, Tampa **Georgia** Emory University, Atlanta □ Life Chiropractic College, Atlanta **Hawaii** University of Hawaii, Honolulu **Illinois** University of Illinois at Urbana-Champaign, Champaign □ Northeastern Illinois University, Chicago □ Northwestern University, Evanston **Indiana** Indiana University, Bloomington **Iowa** Drake University, Des Moines □ University of Osteopathic Medicine, Des Moines **Kansas** Johnson County Community College, Johnson County Kansas State University, Lawrence □ Kansas University of Manhatan, Manhatan □ Washburn University, Topeka **Kentucky** University of Kentucky, Lexington □ University of Louisville, Louisville **Louisiana** Tulane University, New Orleans **Maine** University of Southern Maine, Portland **Maryland** University of Maryland, College Park **Massachusetts** Amherst College, Amherst □ Hampshire College, Amherst □ University of Massachusetts, Amherst □ Berkley School of Music, Boston □ Boston University, Boston □ Brandeis University, Boston □ Emerson College, Boston □ Harvard University, Boston M.I.T., Boston □ Simmons College, Boston □ Smith College, North Hampton □ Mt. Holyoke, S. Hadley □ Clark University, Worcester □ Worcester Poly Tech, Worcester □ Worcester State College, Worcester **Michigan** University of Michigan, Ann Arbor □ Grand Valley State College, Grand Rapids Kalamazoo College, Kalamazoo □ Western Michigan University, Kalamazoo □ Michigan State University, Lansing **Missouri** University of Missouri, Columbia □ Kansas City Art Institute, Kansas City □ University of Missouri, Kansas City □ George Washington University, St. Louis **North Carolina** University of North Carolina, Charlotte **Nebraska** University of Nebraska, Lincoln □ Creighton University, Omaha □ U.N.O., Omaha □ University of Nebraska, Omaha **New Jersey** Middlesex County College, Edison □ Brookdale College, Manalapan □ Atlantic Community College, Mays Landing □ Rutgers University, New Brunswick □ Stockton State College, Pomona □ Princeton University, Princeton □ Fairleigh Dickinson University, Teaneck **New York** S.U.N.Y. University at Albany, Albany □ State University of Binghamton, Binghamton □ S.U.N.Y. University at Binghamton, Binghamton □ State College of Buffalo, Buffalo □ S.U.N.Y. at Buffalo, Buffalo □ Edgate University, Hamilton □ Columbia University, New York City □ New York University, New York City University of Plattsburgh, Plattsburgh □ University of Rochester, Rochester □ University of Syracuse, Syracuse □ Rensselaer Polytechnic Institute, Troy Troy University, Troy **Ohio** Hebrew Union College, Cincinnati □ Miami University of Ohio, Cincinnati □ University of Cincinnati, Cincinnati Case Western University, Cleveland □ Cleveland State University, Cleveland □ Ohio State University, Columbia □ Kent State University, Kent □ Oberlin College, Oberlin □ Bowling Green University, Toledo □ Medical College of Toledo, Toledo □ University of Toledo, Toledo, **Oklahoma** University of Oklahoma, Norman □ Oklahoma State University, Stillwater **Oregon** Lewis & Clark College, Portland □ Portland State University, Portland □ Reed College, Portland **Pennsylvania** University of Westchester, Westchester □ Drexel University, Philadelphia □ Haverford University, Philadelphia □ Penn State University, Philadelphia □ Temple University, Philadelphia □ University of Pittsburgh, Pittsburgh **Rhode Island** Brown University, Providence □ Johnson and Wales, Providence □ Rhode Island School of Design, Providence **South Carolina** University of South Carolina, Columbia **Texas** University of Texas, Austin □ University of Texas, El Paso □ Baylor College of Medicine, Houston □ Rice University, Houston □ Texas Medical Center, Houston University of Houston, Houston □ University of Texas, San Antonio **Virginia** Eastern Virginia Medical Center □ University of Virginia, Charlottesville □ Old Dominion University, Norfolk □ Virginia Commonwealth University, Richmond □ William & Mary, Williamsburg **Vermont** University of Vermont, Burlington **Washington** University of Washington, Seattle **Wisconsin** University of Wisconsin, Madison **Australia** University of New England, Armandale □ Mecqurie University, Sydney □ New S. Wales Institute of Technology, Sydney □ Sydney University, Sydney □ Chisolm University, Melbourne □ La Trobe University, Melbourne □ Melbourne University, Melbourne □ Monash University, Melbourne □ Swinbarne Toch University, Melbourne **Austria** University of Vienna, Vienna **Belgium** Brussels University, Brussels **Brazil** Faap University of San Paulo, San Paulo □ Getulio Vargas University of San Paulo, San Paulo □ Makenzi University of San Paulo, San Paulo □ Maua University of San Paulo, San Paulo □ Pontifical University of San Paulo, San Paulo □ University of San Paulo, San Paulo **Canada** University of Muncton, Muncton □ University of Manitoba, Winnipeg, Manitoba University of Winnipeg, Winnipeg, Manitoba □ Dalhousie University, Halifax, Nova Scotia □ McMaster University, Hamilton, Ontario □ Carlton University, Ottawa, Ontario □ Ottawa University, Ottawa, Ontario □ University of Western Ontario, London, Ontario □ University of Toronto, Toronto, Ontario □ Concordia University, Montreal, Quebec, □ Dawson College, Montreal, Quebec □ McGill University, Montreal, Quebec □ University of Montreal, Montreal, Quebec □ Vanier College, Montreal, Quebec **England** University of Sussex, Brighton □ Cambridge University, Cambridge □ London University, London □ Oxford University, Oxford **France** Caques University, Aix en Provience □ Estullan University, Aix en Provience Le Gazelles University, Aix en Provience □ Faculte de Medecine, Nice □ Facultee de Droit, Nice □ Lycee Massena, Nice □ Bichat University, Paris □ Bobigny University, Paris □ S. Antoine, Paris □ S. Pere, Paris □ Ville Tenz University, Paris □ Voltaire University, Paris **Holland** Amsterdam University, Amsterdam □ Delst University, Delst □ Utrecht University, Utrecht **Israel** Bar Ilan University, Tel Aviv □ Ben Gurion University, Beersheba □ Hebrew University, Jerusalem □ Tel-Aviv University, Tel Aviv **Italy** University of Bologna, Bologna □ University of Ferrara, Ferrara □ University of Fienna, Fienna □ University of Padaua, Padaua □ University of Trieste, Trieste **South Africa** University of Durban, Durban □ University of Witwatersrand, Johannesburg **Spain** Instituta Ibero Americano, Madrid □ Universidad Complutense de Madrid, Madrid □ University of Salamanca, Salamanca Segovin Program for American Students, Segovin □ Toledo Program for American Students, Toledo

"Today there are hundreds of Chabad Houses for students on or near college campuses around the world; they have saved tens of thousands of our children from inter-marriage and have brought many more back to Jewish commitment."

Inset, below: Tefillin on campus— an increasingly familiar sight.

Supplement:
Local Activities
And
Institutions

Chabad-Lubavitch In Michigan:

Education: In Michigan, Chabad-Lubavitch stresses Jewish *education* at all levels, from tots in Kindergarten and Nursery, to pupils in Elementary, Junior and High School, to University students, young married couples and seniors. The Cheder Day-School *(Oholei Yosef Yitschak Lubavitch)* housed in the Jack and Miriam Shenkman Education Center in Farmington Hills, brings the sweetness of Torah to children as young as three! By four they read Hebrew, by six they begin study of *Chumash* (in the original, of course) and by eight *Mishna* and Talmud!

All Chabad Houses provide Judaic instruction at all levels, and the Nursery and pre-1A in Grand Rapids have an educational impact upon two-thirds of the city's Jewish children.

Camps: During the summer, 175 boys and 175 girls enjoy a season of recreation, inspiration and education in two separate sessions on the 660 acres of Camp Gan Israel/Esther Allan in Kalkaska. Flint and Toledo have winter camps, and Grand Rapids runs an outstandingly successful summer day-camp.

Universities: The Schaver-Lazaroff Student Center on the University of Michigan campus in Ann Arbor is the "flagship" of Lubavitch centers catering to the college campus. Other schools serviced include MSU in East Lansing, WMU (Kalamazoo), U of M Extension (Flint), Grand Valley State (Grand Rapids), Medical College (Toledo), and Bowling Green University (near Toledo).

Classes and Lectures: The Irwin I. Cohn Memorial Lecture Series in Talmudic Law features three yearly lectures for lawyers and judges with speakers of national renown. Chairman is Federal Judge Avern Cohn of the U.S. Sixth District Court; Committee members are Judges Hilda Gage, Charles Kaufman, Richard Kaufman, Nathan Kaufman, Charles Levin, Joseph Pernick, John Shepherd, Michael Stacey and Helene White. Classes and Lectures for doctors, lawyers and other professionals are also provided by the Chabad Houses of Toledo, Flint and West Bloomfield.

Mitzva Services: Around the State, Lubavitch distributes *sh'mura matzot* at Passover, *shallach manot* food-gift packages by the thousands at Purim, *menoras* at Chanuka and *lulav/etrog* kits at Sukot. The *shofar* is sounded for the bedridden on Rosh Hashana, and Lubavitch volunteers regularly visit Jewish patients at Harper, Grace, Providence, Beaumont and Botsford Hospitals in Southeast Michigan — and likewise all area hospitals in Ann Arbor, Flint, Grand Rapids and Toledo. A Chaplaincy service is

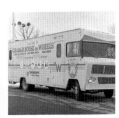

A. The Jack and Miriam Shenkman Lubavitch Education Center, on Middlebelt Road, in Farmington Hills.
B. Oak Park Lubavitch Center, on Nine Mile Road.
C. Seymour and Martha Goldman Congregation Beth Chabad of Farmington Hills, on Middlebelt Road.
D. Bais Chabad Torah Center of West Bloomfield, on Maple Road.
E. Entrance to the newly-dedicated Arlene and Rose Lando Chabad House of Western Michigan, in Grand Rapids, with its Director, Rabbi Yosef Y. Weingarten.
F. Lazaroff-Schaver Student Center; University of Michigan Chabad House in Ann Arbor.
G. Inauguration of "Lubavitch Town" — a proposed educational complex to arise on a forty-acre parcel on Maple Road in West Bloomfield, adjacent to the Jewish Community Center. From left to right, Rabbis Yosef Y. Shemtov, Aaron Y. Goldstein, Berel Shemtov, Yosef Y. Gourarie, Yitschak A. Mann (partially concealed), Yosef Y. Keselman, Bentsion Stein, Chaim M. Bergstein, Elimelech Silberberg, Moshe Zaklikofsky, Yitschak M. Kagan, Shimon Druk, Herschel Finman.

Inset below:
A quiet chess game in Camp Gan Israel/Esther Allan, Kalkaska, Michigan.

A.

B.

C.

D.

ARLENE & ROSE LANDO
CHABAD HOUSE

E.

F.

LUBAVITCH TOWN
INAUGURATION
CHANUKAH 5749
313-737-7000

G.

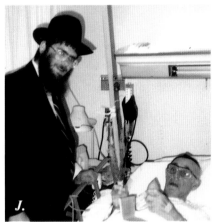

I. Rabbi Yosef Yitschak Keselman, Community Outreach Director, conducts a Chanuka candle-lighting ceremony.

J. Rabbi Yisroel Weingarten, Director of the Flint Chabad House, visiting a hospital patient on Sukot.

K. January 18, 1987. One of the Irwin I. Cohn Memorial Talmudic Law lectures. From left to right: Chairman of the session, Hon. John Shepherd, Judge on the Michigan Court of Appeals; the lecturer — Rabbi Dr. J. David Bleich, Hon. Charles Kaufman, Judge on the Wayne County Circuit Court; Hon. George Brody, Judge on the Federal Bankruptcy Court; Dr. Norman Rosenzweig, Head of Psychiatry, Sinai Hospital; Dr. Jason Bodzin, Chief of Surgery, Mt. Carmel Hospital; Dr. Lawrence Baker, Oncology Dept., WSU Medical School; Dr. Mark Evans, Professor of Obstetrics and Gynecology, WSU Medical School; Hon. Ira Kaufman, Wayne County; Dr. Michael H. Lehmann, associate Professor of Medicine, Wayne State University and Director of Electrophysiology Laboratories and Arrhythmia Service, Harper Hospital; Hon. Avern Cohn, Judge on the Federal Court (U.S. Sixth District) and Chairman of the Lecture Series.

L. Girls' session, Camp Gan Israel/Esther Allan, Kalkaska, Michigan

Inset below:
Rabbi Yosef Y. Shemtov, director of Chabad House of Toledo, Ohio, leading a children's rally.

maintained at Milan Penitentiary and Kent County Prison. Lubavitch Women's Organization holds weekly classes for seniors at Highland Towers Apartments, and holiday visits to the Federation Apartments and local nursing homes.

Pushkeh, Counselling, and Drug Prevention: Nine thousand families have a regularly serviced Lubavitch *Pushkeh* (charity box). Marriage and personal counselling is an on-going service, and Chabad of Farmington Hills is a fully-authorized branch of the renowned national program for drug-abuse prevention called "P.R.I.D.E." Chabad House on Wheels reaches Jewish families as far north as the Upper Peninsula.

"Lubavitch Town": This unique educational complex will be built on forty acres of land (just acquired by the Lubavitch Foundation) on Maple Road in West Bloomfield, adjoining the Jewish Community Center. Institutions planned for the site are a Rabbinical College, a Day-Care Center, a Torah Public Library, Retreat Center, Seminar for Seniors, and a Day Camp.

Directory:

Chabad Lubavitch Michigan Headquarters

28555 Middlebelt Road Farmington Hills Michigan 48018 (313) 737-7000

Regional Director
Rabbi Berel Shemtov

Associate Director
Rabbi Yitschak M. Kagan

Education Outreach Director
Rabbi Herschel Finman

Camp Gan Israel/Esther Allan Director
Mrs. Berel Shemtov

Cheder Day-School Director
Rabbi Bentsiyon Stein

Rosh Yeshiva
Rabbi Yosef Y. Gourarie

Senior Staff
Rabbi Shimon Druk,
Rabbi David Nussbaum

Lubavitch Center of Oak Park
14000 W. Nine Mile Road
Oak Park, Michigan 48237
(313) 543-6611

Congregation Mishkan Israel
Nusach H'Ari

Hospital Visitation Director
Rabbi Moshe Zaklikofsky

Community Outreach Director
Rabbi Yosef Y. Keselman

Family Visitation & Pushkeh Division Director
Rabbi Yitschak A. Mann

Chabad House on Wheels Director
Rabbi Hershel Zaklos

Congregation Beth Chabad of Farmington Hills
Seymour & Martha Goldman Center
32000 Middlebelt Road
Farmington Hills
Michigan 48018
(313) 626-3194
Rabbi Chayim M. Bergstein
Project Pride — Drug Abuse Prevention
Dial-A-Jewish Story

Bais Chabad Torah Center of West Bloomfield
5595 W. Maple Road
West Bloomfield
Michigan 48033
(313) 855-6170
Rabbi Elimelech Silberberg
A.I. Morrison Library
Mikva

Bloomfield Hills Program;
Rabbi Moshe Y. Polter
399-3918

University of Michigan Chabad House
Lazaroff-Schaver Student Center
715 Hill Street
Ann Arbor
Michigan 48104
(313) 769-3078
Rabbi Aharon Y. Goldstein
(313) 99-LEARN

Chabad House of Eastern Michigan
5944 Oak Tree Drive
Flint, Michigan 48504
(313) 733-3779
Rabbi Yisrael Weingarten
Also serving Lapeer, Port Huron, Bay City, Saginaw, Midland

Chabad House of Western Michigan
Arlene & Rose Lando Center
2615 Michigan Avenue NE
Grand Rapids
Michigan 49503
(616) 957-0770
Rabbi Yosef Y. Weingarten
Also serving Kalamazoo, Benton Harbor, Muskegon, Grandhaven, Holland

Camp Gan Israel/ Esther Allan
Route 1, Box 272, Lake Valley Road, Kalkaska
Michigan 49646
(616) 258-9824
Boys' Season — July
Girls' Season — August

Chabad House of Toledo
2350 Secor
Toledo, Ohio 43606
(419) 535-1930
Rabbi Yosef Y. Shemtov

*Inset below:
Chanuka, 1987. A team of Lubavitch rabbinical students visits the tiny, isolated communities in the Upper Peninsula.*

Main Photo:
College and university
students from
around the U.S. and
Canada come to
the "Encounter with
Chabad" weekends
arranged by the Luba-
vitch Youth Organ-
ization in New York.
Here, a Chabad
sh'liach, Rabbi
Sholom Wineberg
(of Kansas City,
Missouri) is engaged
in a heated discussion
following one of
the "Encounter" main
sessions.
Inset, below:
A student brings music
to a Chabad House.

The Chabad House

A Chabad House is a Jewish community center in the truest sense of the term—
the nerve center of all the educational and outreach activities of the Chabad-Lubavitch lamplighter,
serving the needs of the entire Jewish community, from the youngsters of Tzivos Hashem to
the elderly, and everyone in-between. The Rebbe has called for the expansion of activities in existing
Chabad Houses, and the establishment of new Chabad-Lubavitch centers wherever Jews live,
in the cities, in the suburbs, on college campuses throughout the nation and around the world.
And his representatives are responding with renewed energy to the Rebbe's call.

In 1972, in a letter written on the occasion of the opening of a new Chabad House, the Rebbe extended
his prayerful wish that the new institution should serve as a key to open the hearts of all who
will visit it, and all who will come under its sphere of influence—open their hearts to the very core
of their Jewishness. Of this innermost core, it has been said that it is always "awake" and
responsive, regardless of the outer layers encrusting it. And when the inner core of the heart is touched,
it reveals the very essence of the Jew, permeating him with the Torah, *Torat Chaim,* and the
mitzvot whereby Jews live, so that he becomes an inspiration to others.

In the Chabad Houses, and in all their activities, the *sh'luchim* are Abraham's heirs.
They have inherited his kindness and compassion, his selfless commitment to the cause of making
G-d known in the world, and revealing G-dliness every place on earth. They will not rest
until the wellsprings of Torah have spread forth everywhere, "..to the West, and to the East,
and to the North, and to the South."

Main Photo:
*Chabad House school
and Yeshiva Gedolah,
Yeoville, Johannes-
burg, South Africa.*
Inset, below:
*Chabad House
and Lubavitch Retreat
Center, Richmond,
Virginia, U.S.A.*

Torah-Teacher To The World

Torah Scholarship: In the world of Torah-study, Torah-knowledge and Torah-research, Chabad-Lubavitch excels. Its senior *yeshivot* and its *kolel* institutions are renowned for their eminent standards of scholarship; each publishes weekly bulletins of commentaries and discussions by pupils and faculty, and a monthly, quarterly, or biannual research journal with learned articles on Jewish Law, Talmud and Chassidism. *Or Hadorom* ("Light from the South"), for example, published by the Lubavitch institutions of higher learning in Australia, has earned a reputation as one of the most important Torah journals today. In all, *over three thousand* such bulletins and journals have appeared in print.

Then there is the rabbinate: Throughout all of Europe, Israel, Africa, Australia and North America, Lubavitch chassidim and graduates of Chabad institutions occupy prominent rabbinical positions.

The Inspiration: The impetus and inspiration for these achievements is provided by the Rebbe, who motivates effort, toil and an aspiration to excel, on two fronts—personal growth in learning, and teaching Torah to others. He motivates not only by urging and instructing, but also by personal example. The Rebbe is, simply stated, the greatest Torah-scholar of our age, both in Talmud and Jewish law, as well as in the esoteric depths of *kabbala* and Chassidism. He has shown through a lifetime of teaching the intimate connections between the "revealed" and "hidden" Torah, between the practical rules of Jewish law and the truths of Jewish mysticism or, more correctly, of Chassidism. *Some one hundred volumes have been published of the Rebbe's talks and writings.* Central among them are the twenty-six volumes of *Likuttei Sichot,* an anthology of the talks relating to the weekly sections of the Torah and special occasions in the Jewish Calendar. In addition, eight volumes of his letters—containing new Torah insights—have been published recently,

The Rebbe:
A. On the reviewing stand of the central Lag B'Omer Parade at 770 Eastern Parkway, Brooklyn, N.Y., acknowledging the salute of a passing float and one group of the 25,000 youthful marchers.
B. At the microphone addressing a major farbrengen.
C. In conversation.
D. Giving nickels to young children for them to place into a pushkeh (charity coin-box).

and a further (approximately) thirty volumes are being prepared for publication.

The Teacher: The Rebbe is Torah-teacher to the world, educating each person according to his level and outlook. He deepens the knowledge and broadens the intellectual horizons of the *talmid chacham,* the scholar. To the chassid, whether scholarly or simple, he teaches and imparts— in addition to knowledge—self-discipline and dedication. To the child or the unlearned individual, the Rebbe gets his educational message across by *inspiration,* inspiring them to higher levels of good conduct and moral living. To the non-Jewish population the Rebbe brings a message of ethical guidance in light of Torah, and he evokes their utter respect as sage, teacher, and leader.

The Farbrengen: What is the "classroom," the medium of interaction? Primarily it is the *farbrengen,* a Torah-gathering in the chassidic spirit, in which the Rebbe speaks to the public. The mood and atmosphere is an indescribable mix of joy, brotherhood, warmth, liveliness…and earnest concentration.

On almost every Shabbat, and many other weekday occasions, the Rebbe conducts a *farbrengen* at which he speaks for several hours, teaching subjects which range from the profoundest analysis of the weekly Torah-reading to the most penetrating, systematic, and innovative examination of talmudic and chassidic thought. Some four to five thousand attend the weekly shabbat *farbrengens,* many more on special occasions.

Among the huge crowds in attendance at a *farbrengen* at Lubavitch World Headquarters in New York, one can find people from all walks of life, young and old, professors, scientists, government officials, men of the arts, professionals and plain folk.

"Hook-Up"; Telephone and Satellite: When the Rebbe speaks on weekdays his talk is transmitted live via satellite to cable TV stations across North America and parts of South America,

"With a drop of wine and an ocean of love, from the Torah-teacher of the world."

*Inset below:
Giving nickels
to young children for
them to place
into a pushkeh
(charity coin-box).*

Main Photo:
Part of the sophisti-
cated electronic
telephone control
board in the World
Lubavitch Communi-
cations Center,
which broadcasts the
Rebbe's public
weekday addresses,
via satellite, to Radio
Stations and Chabad-
Lubavitch Centers
around the globe.

and often to Israel, Europe, Africa and Australia, bringing the Rebbe into millions of Jewish and non-Jewish homes. A special telephone hookup system also relays the talks live to Lubavitch Centers around the world. A simultaneous English translation of his talk in Yiddish is provided for the television audience. Those personally attending the *farbrengen* can use wireless receivers providing simultaneous translations in English, Hebrew, Spanish, French and other languages.

The Maimonides Study Campaign: The monumental *Mishneh Torah* of Maimonides encompasses all Jewish law. In 1984 the Rebbe initiated the idea that this encyclopedic code should be studied day by day, to be completed every year. Hundreds of thousands of people—from children to accomplished scholars—are united in this daily study. The annual celebration of the *siyum*, when the *Mishneh Torah* is completed and begun anew, has become a pre-eminent occasion on the calendar, when public gatherings of scholars take place on every continent.

"One hundred volumes have been published of the Rebbe's talks and writings. Central among them are the twenty-six volumes of Likuttei Sichot."

Impact and History: But what of the impact? What of the unprecedented historial significance? *I receive an intense, high-level lecture for over four hours, each week, from the leader of the generation, in Talmud, in Torah-law and in* kabbala. *Even more, I am being taught a* method *in Talmud study, a* system *in analyzing the scriptural commentary of Rashi, a unified conceptual approach to all of Torah. And the sheer scope of it! Do you realize that after Shabbat, several scholars, gifted with exceptional memory, review and record the Rebbe's talks (they could not take notes during the* farbrengen, *since writing is prohibited on Shabbat). Later, the Torah-discourses are transcribed and communicated round the world, and on Sunday (Monday in Australia), you will find scholars excitedly discussing the previous* *day's sichot (farbrengen-talks) in Jerusalem, Safed and Paris, in Casablanca, Leeds, Amsterdam*

and Johannesburg. I tell you, the very thought of it evokes awe, absolute awe...

Or you could look at it another way. Think of lights going on around the world:

It is 9:30 p.m. in Brooklyn, New York, on a weekday night. The Rebbe's farbrengen, at 770 Eastern

Parkway, has just begun. In London, England it is 2:30 a.m., after midnight. But the lights are

on in Lubavitch House, and the chassidim are straining to concentrate on the Rebbe's words. In Israel,

it is 4:30 a.m., but the lights are on in Kfar Chabad, and most of the town is up—gathered in the

central shul for the hook-up with New York...

Video to the World Community: The *farbrengen* is over. In New York it is past midnight.

The phones at Lubavitch World Headquarters are still ringing. Many non-Jews are among the callers.

They have been glued to their screens for the past few hours, from Maine to California,

unable to tear themselves away from the unusual, radiant face of a Jewish rabbi. They have listened

to the Rebbe's serious discussion of education, of morality, of ethics, of the belief in one G-d.

The callers are full of questions. "Who is the rabbi?" "What is Lubavitch?" And throughout their

phone conversations run sentiments of *respect* and admiration; as one caller put it,

"I didn't know the Jewish People still have such great sages."

A Drop of Wine: Another *farbrengen* is over, this time at the close of the Shavuot holiday.

It is, once again, past midnight, but no-one would ever guess that. Cars are pulling up outside "770."

They are here to receive *kos shel bracha,* wine from the "cup of blessing" over which grace-

"When the Rebbe speaks on weekdays his talk is transmitted live via satellite to cable TV stations across North America and parts of South America, and often to Israel, Europe, Africa and Australia."

Inset, below: "L'chayim" to the Rebbe!

after-meals has been said by the Rebbe. (From ancient times it has been part of Jewish tradition to give from this wine to family, friends, etc.) They have come from all the Jewish neighborhoods in New York; from Boro Park, Flatbush, Bensonhurst, Kew Gardens and Far Rockaway. Some from as far as New Jersey, Connecticut, Pennsylvania and Massachusetts. From every affiliation, chassidic, orthodox, and non-observant. Inside, a never-ending stream of humanity files past the Rebbe's table. The Rebbe, on his feet the entire time, pours a little wine from his constantly-refilled kiddush-cup into the outstretched cups of those passing by. To their murmured *l'chayim* toast the Rebbe responds, *l'chayim velivracha,* "for life and for blessing."

The lines continue. It is now 4 a.m. The Rebbe is still on his feet. Bear in mind that the Rebbe, in his eighties—he should have long, healthy years—had just concluded four hours of intense Torah-talks, before beginning *kos shel bracha!* His energy, his smile, is unflagging. As he pours into the last few cups outstretched to him, with his other hand he motions rhythmically to the crowd to continue their singing, to increase volume and tempo.

"They have been glued to their screens for the past few hours, from Maine to California, unable to tear themselves away from the unusual, radiant face of a Jewish rabbi."

It is 4:15 a.m. *More than ten thousand cups have been poured by the Rebbe's hand!*

A night has passed, and the lives of tens of thousands of people have been touched. Intellectually. Inspirationally. Educationally. Spiritually. Religiously. With a drop of wine and an ocean of love, from the Torah-teacher of the world.

Main Photo:
4:00 a.m. Brooklyn,
New York, U.S.A.,
770 Eastern Parkway.
Kos shel bracha;
the Rebbe pouring
little cups of wine from
the traditional "cup
of blessing," for thou-
sands of people.

The Publications Of Chabad-Lubavitch

אימתי קאתי מר לכשיפוצו
מעינותיך חוצה
(נסמן בלקו״ש ח״ב ע׳ 468)

When will the master (Mashiach, the Messiah) come? When the wellsprings of your (the Baal Shem Tov's) teachings will spread to the outside. (See Likuttei Sichos, Vol. 2, p. 468)

It began soon after the present Rebbe escaped Nazi-occupied Europe and arrived in the United States on 28 Sivan (June 23), 1941.

His father-in-law, the previous Rebbe, Rabbi Yosef Yitzchak Schneersohn, had arrived just over a year before—physically broken from his experiences first in Bolshevik jail and later under the Nazi occupation of Poland. But his spirit remained invincible. Although the United States was then, from a Torah perspective, a spiritual wasteland, he immediately announced his intention of turning North America into a fortress of Torah, and one of his first acts was to establish Kehot Publication Society. KeHoT is an acronym for *Karnei Hod Torah*—"The Glorious Rays of Torah." And that precisely describes its work, illuminating the Jewish world with books that reflect the full radiance of our holy Torah.

Since then, Kehot and its subsidiary, *Otsar HaChassidim—Sifriyat Lubavitch* ("Treasure-House Of The Chassidim—Library Of Lubavitch") have issued over 1250 titles, besides thousands of magazines and brochures. Kehot pioneered the publishing of Torah literature on all readership levels, in Hebrew, Yiddish, English, and a dozen other languages, spreading "the glorious rays of Torah" to the furthest corners of the world.

The Revolution: First publication to come off the Kehot press—in time for Chanuka, 1942—was "Talks and Tales," the world's first Torah-oriented children's monthly. The periodical has continued uninterrupted publication up to the present for 47 years, now throughout the world in many languages. Also among the first English-language publications were a popular series of Jewish history books, "Our People," written from a pure Torah perspective; also "The Festival Series," "The Complete Story of Tishrei," etc. which made Jewish holidays and practices come alive for children and adults. Then there were the story books, "The Adopted Princess," "The Secret Code," etc.,

111

Main Photo:
Talks and writings
of the Rebbe.

Main Sets are:
Top shelf and center
of second shelf:
Sichot Kodesh, trans-
cripts of farbrengen-
talks; 49 volumes.

Second shelf, left:
Igrot Kodesh, letters;
8 volumes published,
and a further
30 volumes
(approximately)
being prepared for
publication.

Third Shelf:
Likuttei Sichot,
27 volumes.

Bottom Shelf:
Sichos In English,
27 volumes.

all containing inspiring tales of Jewish heroism in adverse circumstances of our past and present. All these and many more breathed new spirit into the American Jewish community, who had been deprived—until Kehot's founding—of suitable literature in their language. For the thousands of youth now enrolled in the *yeshivot* that began to spring up around the land, Kehot publications were an essential reinforcement—and they were avidly read by tens of thousands more, who were not fortunate enough to receive a day-school education, but who were inspired by these books to become more aware of their Jewish identity and committed to it in practice.

The revolution in popular English-language Torah-publications that Kehot initiated in the 1940s, caught on, and, several decades later, sparked an enormous expansion of similar publications by commercial publishing companies.

Chassidic Philosophy: All seven Rebbes of Chabad-Lubavitch were among the most prolific and original expounders of Torah ideas in Jewish history. The vast collection of their written works, and oral discourses recorded by their followers, constitutes the most remarkable treasure-house of comprehensive Torah philosophy produced in the past few centuries.

Unfortunately, until a decade or two ago, it was also the most unrecognized. Before World War I, not more than 25 works of Chabad philosophy had been published—a tiny portion of the total literary output. The present Rebbe began the difficult task of preparing these manuscripts for publication in the early 1940s. The tempo successively increased in decades following, as an increasing number of these unpublished manuscripts were brought to light. To date over 500 volumes of Chabad philosophy have been published, most of them hefty volumes, and expert research teams are hard at work preparing the rest for publication.

"Kehot publications... were avidly read by tens of thousands... who were inspired by these books to become more aware of their Jewish identity and committed to it in practice."

Main Photo:
A small selection from
the publications
of Kehot Publication
Society.

Tapes…and Tanya: The scope of Chabad-Lubavitch publications is wide-ranging: Judaic thought and philosophy; Torah-law; chassidism; numerous volumes to and about the Jewish woman; musically annotated Chabad melodies—with a history of chassidic music; for children— a host of beautifully illustrated volumes on holidays, customs, stories and history; schoolbooks and textbooks for formal study; thousands of audio cassettes with recorded lessons on Maimonides, chassidism, philosophy and other subjects. And then, of course, there is the historically unprecedented publishing of the *Tanya* (basic work of Chabad Chassidism), at the Rebbe's special request, *over 3000 times,* in cities large and small around the globe, from Shanghai, China to Harare, Zimbabwe, and from the island of Djerba (off Tunisia) to the Suez Canal, wherever even one single Jew was found. The spiritual and psychological uplift derived from the identification of each community with *its own edition* of Tanya—has been incalculable.

It should be noted that Kehot's 1,250 titles do not include the thousands of booklets of Torah explanations published weekly or periodically by Lubavitch educational institutions around the world, besides booklets published by local Chabad Houses and centers. Also noteworthy is that many of these works had to be republished several times. *It is estimated that Kehot and its international branches have printed over 100 million volumes and booklets in the course of the past 45 years, an achievement utterly without parallel in the entire history of Jewish publishing.*

As "the glorious rays of Torah" have spread, they have illuminated the world with their light, warmed the Jewish people with their fire. Millions are now more Torah-knowledgeable and Torah-observant as a result of their beneficial influence.

It is difficult to imagine how the Jewish world would have looked without them.

"It is estimated that Kehot and its international branches have printed over 100 million volumes and booklets in the course of the past 45 years."

Inset, below: A small representative selection of the Hebrew-language pamphlets published by Chabad-Lubavitch of Israel, who have disseminated over nine million such brochures!

Main Photo:
A librarian in the rare-
book section of
the Agudas Chassidei
Chabad library
and archive center at
World Lubavitch
Headquarters.

Glossary

ahavat yisrael: Love of fellow Jew

avoda: Service (of G-d); striving

baalei teshuva: Repentants, returnees to Jewish practice

Beit hamikdash: The Holy Temple in Jerusalem

bina: Comprehension, grasp; second stage of intellect

Chabad: An acrostic formed from the initial letters of the words *Cho*chma, ("wisdom"), *Bi*na ("comprehension"), *Da*'at ("knowledge")

chassid: (plural: **chassidim**): Follower of the Rebbe, adherent of the chassidic life style

chazzan: Reader (or cantor) leading the synagogue services

cheder: Torah-school for young children

chumash: Pentateuch

etrog: Citron fruit used on Sukot

farbreng: (verb): To gather in the chassidic spirit.

farbrengen: Chassidic gathering

gemilut chassadim: Beneficence; charity

hachnassat orchim: Hospitality

halacha: Torah law

haggada: Passover book for the Seder

Hashem: G-d

illuy: Prodigy or genius in Torah-scholarship

kabbala: "Inner" esoteric depths of Torah; mysticism

kashrut: Observance of the kosher laws; dietary propriety of foods by Torah law

kiddush: Prayer over wine introducing Shabbat and festivals

kittel: White robe, worn for prayer on Yom Kippur

kolel: Institute of advanced Torah studies for married men

kos shel bracha: "Cup of blessing"; cup of wine over which Grace-after-meals has been said

Lag B'Omer: 33rd day of the Omer; a festival

Lubavitch: a town in White Russia, center of the Chabad-Lubavitch chassidic movement for over a century

lulav: Date-palm branch used on Sukot

Mashiach: Messiah

megilla: Scroll of Esther, read on Purim

menora: Eight-branched candelabrum for the Chanuka Festival

mezuza: Parchment-scroll, inscribed with two paragraphs of Torah; affixed to doorpost

mikva (plural: **mikva'ot):** Immersion pool built to rigid specifications of Torah-law; used primarily by married women as part of "Family Purity" laws

mitzva (plural: mitzvot): Precept or command of Torah

neshama: Soul

o.b.m.: Of blessed memory

pikuach nefesh: Danger to life

pushkeh: Charity coin-bank

Rebbe (plural: **Rebbe'im**): leader and head of the chassidim

Sefer Torah: The sacred Torah-scroll, inscribed with the Pentateuch

shallach manot: Contracted form of **mishloach manot**, Purim food-gifts

sh'liach: (Plural: **sh'luchim** male): Emissary

sh'lita: Acrostic; **Sheyichyeh Leyamim Tovim Aruchim**; "May he live for long happy years."

sh'lucha: (plural: **sh'luchot** female): Emissary

sh'ma: The "Hear-O-Israel" prayer

shmura matzo: Passover matzos, hand made from specially guarded wheat

shofar: Ram's horn, sounded on Rosh Hashana

shul: Synagogue

shtetl: Jewish communities in pre-World War II Europe

sichot: Discourses delivered by the Rebbe

siddur: Prayer book

siyum: Celebration marking the completion of study of a book or tractate of Torah teachings

suka: Outdoor structures used on Sukot

Sukot: Tabernacles (Festival of)

taharat hamishpacha: "Family Purity"; See **mikva**

tallit: Prayer-shawl

talmid chacham: Torah-scholar

Tanya: Source-text of Chabad; authored by Rabbi Schneur Zalman of Liadi (1745-1812)

tefilla: Prayer

tefillin: Phylacteries

teshuva: Repentance, return

Torah: The overall body of Jewish religious teachings, scriptural and rabbinic

tzedaka: Charity

yahrzeit: Anniversary of the passing

yeshiva: School of Torah-study

yetzer hara: The inner inclination to evil

yiddishkeit: Torah-Judaism

Yisrael: Lit. "Israel"; The Jewish People

yomtov: Festival

Directory Of Chabad-Lubavitch Centers

ופרצת ימה וקדמה צפנה
ונגבה

(בראשית כח, יד)

And you shall spread forth to the west and to the east, to the north and to the south.
(Genesis 28:14)

Chabad-Lubavitch World Headquarters, 770 Eastern Parkway, Brooklyn, New York, U.S.A.

World Headquarters
Agudas Chassidei Chabad
Merkos L'Inyonei Chinuch
Machne Israel
770 Eastern Parkway
Brooklyn, New York 11213
718-493-9250

Tzeirei Agudas Chabad
Lubavitch Youth Organization
718-953-1000

Note: Many centers listed below have branch offices. For information call World HQ or nearest city office.

U.S.A.

Alabama

Rabbi Y. Lipszyc
Chabad House
2025 University Blvd.
Birmingham, AL 35233
205-328-6724

Arizona

Rabbi Z. Levertov
Chabad Lubavitch
of Arizona
1536 E. Maryland
Phoenix, AZ 85014
602-274-5377

Rabbi Y. Shemtov
Chabad Lubavitch
of Tucson
1301 East Elm
Tucson, AZ 85719
602-881-7955-6

California

Rabbi S. D. Raichik
Chabad-Lubavitch
101 N. Edinburgh Avenue
Los Angeles, CA 90048
213-931-0913

Rabbi B. S. Cunin
Chabad West Coast
Headquarters
741 Gayley Avenue
Los Angeles, CA 90024
213-208-7511

Rabbi M. Bryski
Chabad of Agoura
368 North Kanan Road
Agoura, CA 91301
818-991-0991

Rabbi Y. Lazar
Chabad of Anaheim Hills
1265 N. Schrisdey #A203
Anaheim Hills, CA 92807
714-693-0770

Rabbi C. Mentz
Chabad of Bel Air
10421 Summer Holly Circle
Bel Air, CA 90077
213-475-5311

Rabbi Y. Langer
Chabad of Berkeley
2340 Piedmont Avenue
Berkeley, CA 94704
415-540-5824

Rabbi Y. Shusterman
Chabad of Beverly Hills
409 North Foothill
Beverly Hills, CA 90210
213-859-3948

Rabbi B. Hecht
Chabad of Brentwood
11920 S. Vincente Blvd.
#208
Brentwood, CA 90049
213-826-4453

Rabbi A. Begun
Chabad of Cheviot Hills
3355 Manning Avenue #17
Chevoit Hills, CA 90064
213-837-4941

Rabbi Y. Gordon
Chabad of the Valley
4915 Hayvenhurst
Encino, CA 91436
818-784-9985

Rabbi M. Bryski
Chabad of Granada Hills
10349 Balboa Blvd. #204
Granada Hills, CA 91344
818-784-9985

Rabbi A. Berkowitz
Chabad of West
Orange County
5702 Clark Drive #18
Huntington Beach,
CA 92649
714-846-2285

Rabbi M. Duchman
Chabad of Irvine
Jewish Center
4872 Royce Road
Irvine, CA 97215
714-786-5000

Rabbi A. Tennenbaum
Chabad of Laguna
P.O.B. 253
Laguna Beach, CA 92652
714-786-5000

Rabbi E. Hecht
Chabad of South Bay
24412 Narbonne Avenue
Lomita, CA 90717
213-326-8234

Rabbi Y. Newman
Congregation Lubavitch
3981 Atlantic Avenue
Long Beach, CA 90807
213-434-6338

Rabbi Y. Marcus
Chabad of Los Alamitos
10412 El Dorado
Los Alamitos, CA 90720
213-594-6408

Chabad Drug
Rehabilitation Center
1952 S. Robertson
Los Angeles, CA 90034
213-204-3196

Rabbi Y. Mishulovin
Chabad Mid City Center
420 N. Fairfax Avenue
Los Angeles, CA 90046
213-655-9282

Rabbi N. Estulin
Chabad Russian Synagogue
221 S. La Brea
Los Angeles, CA 90036
213-938-1837

Rabbi E. Schochet
Yeshiva Ohr Elchonon
Chabad
7215 Waring Avenue
Los Angeles, CA 90046
213-937-3763

Rabbi S. Naparstek
Chabad of Marina Del Ray
714 Washington Street
Marina Del Ray, CA 90292
213-306-4649

Rabbi M. Shur
Chabad of Pacific Palisades
Pacific Palisades, CA

Rabbi Y. Denenbaum
Chabad of Palm Springs
425 Avenida Ortega
Palm Springs, CA 92262
619-325-0774

Rabbi Y. Levin
Chabad of the Peninsula
3070 Louis Road
Palo Alto, CA 94303
415-424-9800

Rabbi Y. Goldstein
Chabad of Poway
16934 Espola Road
Poway, CA 92064
619-451-0455

Rabbi Y. Goldstein
Chabad of
Rancho Bernardo
11655 Duenda Road #F
Rancho Bernardo,
CA 92127
619-451-0455

Rabbi N. Gross
Chabad of Palos Verdes
777 Silver Spur Road #12B
Rolling Hills Estate,
CA 90274
213-544-5544

Rabbi Y. Loschak
Chabad of S. Barbara
487 N. Turnpike Road
S. Barbara, CA 93111
805-683-1554

Rabbi Y. Fradkin
Chabad of S. Diego
6115 Montezuma Road
S. Diego, CA 92115
619-265-7700

Rabbi M. Lieder
Chabad of La Jolla
3232 Governor Dr.
S. Diego, CA 92122
619-455-1670

Rabbi A. Hecht
Chabad of S. Francisco
3036 Octavia
S. Francisco, CA 94123
415-673-5770

Rabbi A. Levitansky
Chabad of S. Monica
1428 17th Street
S. Monica, CA 90404
213-829-5620

Rabbi C. Dalfin
Chabad of Marin
1150 Loylberry Road
S. Rafael, CA 94913
415-492-1666

Rabbi M. Weiss
Chabad of Sherman Oaks
1463 Ventura Blvd. #202
Sherman Oaks, CA 91423
818-784-9985

Rabbi M. Einbinder
Blauner Youth Center
18211 Burbank Blvd.
Tarzana, CA 92356
818-784-9985

Rabbi A. Abend
Chabad of
North Hollywood
13079 Chandler Blvd.
Van Nuys, CA 91401
818-989-9539

Rabbi Y. Ladowicz
Chabad of Ventura
5850 Thille #101
Ventura, CA 93003
805-658-7441

Rabbi B. Zaltsman
Chabad Lubavitch
Russian Outreach Center
7414 S. Monica Blvd.
West Hollywood, CA 90046
213-874-7583

Rabbi A. Yemini
Chabad Chai Center
of Pico Robertson
Chabad Israeli Center
9017 W. Pico
W. Los Angeles, CA 90035
213-271-6193

Rabbi Y. Sapochkinsky
Chabad of Westlake
741 Lakefield Road #E
Westlake Village, CA 91361
805-497-9635

Rabbi G. Shusterman
Hebrew Academy
Lubavitch Orange County
14401 Willow Lane
Westminster, CA 92683
213-596-1681

Rabbi D. Eliezri
Chabad of Yorba Linda
19045 Yorba Linda Blvd.
Yorba Linda, CA 92686
714-693-0770

Colorado

Rabbi A. Sirota
Chabad Lubavitch
of Boulder
3100 Arapahoe
Boulder, CO 80303
303-440-7772

Rabbi M. Teitelbaum
Chabad Lubavitch
of Colorado Springs
3465 Nonchalant Circle E.
Colorado Springs,
CO 80917
719-596-7330

Rabbi Y. Popack
Chabad Lubavitch
of Colorado
400 S. Holly Street
Denver, CO 80222
303-329-0211

Chabad Lubavitch
of Fort Collins
904 E. Elizabeth Street
Fort Collins, CO 80524
303-484-9971

Connecticut

Rabbi S. Hecht
Chabad Center
of Greater New Haven
566 Whalley Avenue #1B
New Haven, CT 06511
203-397-1111

Rabbi Y. Kalmanson
Yeshiva Gedola
of New Haven
300 Norton
New Haven, CT 06511
203-789-9879

Rabbi M. Hecht
New Haven Hebrew
Day School-Lubavitch
261 Derby Avenue
Orange, CT 06477
203-795-5261

Rabbi Y. Deren
Chabad House
114 Grove Street
Stamford, CT 06901
203-324-3779

Rabbi Y. Gopin
Chabad House
2352 Albany Avenue
West Hartford, CT 06117
203-232-1116

Delaware

Rabbi C. Vogel
Chabad Lubavitch
of Delaware
1306 Grienell Road
Wilmington, DE 19803
302-478-4400

Florida

Rabbi S. Lipskar
Shul of Bal Harbor-Chabad
9701 Collins Avenue
Bal Harbor, FL 33154
305-868-1411

Rabbi Y. Biston
Chabad Lubavitch
19146 Lyons Avenue
Boca Raton, FL 33434
305-344-2778

Rabbi S.B. Dubov
Chabad Center
in Casselberry
1035 E. Semoran Blvd.
Casselberry, FL
407-332-7906

Rabbi Y. Denburg
Chabad Lubavitch
of Broward
8803 Sample Rd.
Coral Springs, FL 33065
305-344-2778

Chabad Lubavitch
Community Center
9791 Sample Road
Coral Springs, FL 33065
305-344-4855

Rabbi M. Schwartz
Chabad House
of South Broward
3339-2 University Drive
Davie, FL 33024
305-437-7770

Rabbi R. Tenenhaus
Congregation
Levi Yitzchok
1295 E. Hallandale
Beach Blvd.
Hallandale, FL 33009
305-458-1877

Rabbi A. Liberman
Synagogue of
Inverrary-Chabad
4561 N. University Drive
Lauderhill, FL 33321
305-748-1777

Rabbi S. Dubow
Chabad House of
Greater Orlando
642 Green Meadow Ave.
Maitland, FL 32751
407-740-8770

Anshei Lubavitch
1613 Alton Road
Miami Beach, FL 33139

Rabbi S. Blank
Congregation Lubavitch
Russian Immigrant Center
1120 Collins Avenue
Miami Beach, FL 33139
305-673-5755

Rabbi L. Shapiro
Congregation Lubavitch
3925 Collins Avenue
Cadillac Hotel
Miami Beach, FL 33180
305-932-9020

Rabbi A. Korf
Merkos Lubavitch
of Florida
1140 Alton Rd.
Miami Beach, FL 33139
305-673-5664

Rabbi Y. Fellig
Lubavitch Foundation
of Coconut Grove
5415 Collins Avenue
Miami Beach, FL 33140
305-866-9003

Rabbi C. Brusowankin
Chabad of North Dade
2590 N.E. 202nd Street
N. Miami Beach, FL 33180
305-932-9029

Chabad of Sarasota
Sarasota, FL 34239

Rabbi Y. Dubrowski
Chabad House
14606 Brentwood Lane
Tampa, FL 33618
813-962-2375

Congregation Bais Tefila
3418 Handy Road
Tampa, FL 33618
813-963-2317

Rabbi S. Ezagui
Chabad Lubavitch
of West Palm Beach
1867 N. Congress
W. Palm Beach, FL 33401
305-683-8180

Georgia

Rabbi Y. New
Congregation Beth Tefilah
5065 High Point Road
Atlanta, GA 30342
404-843-2464

Hawaii

Rabbi Y. Krasnjansky
Chabad of Hawaii
4851 Kahala Avenue
Honolulu, HI 96816
808-735-8161

Illinois

Rabbi D. Moscowitz
Lubavitch Chabad
of Illinois
3107 W. Devon Avenue
Chicago, IL 60659
312-262-2770

Rabbi M. Benhayoun
Lubavitch Chabad
of the Loop
401 S. Lasalle Street
#9-770
Chicago, IL 60605
312-427-7770

Rabbi B. Scheiman
Lubavitch Chabad of Niles
9263 Hamlin Avenue
Des Plaines, IL 60016
312-296-1770

Rabbi D. Klein
Tannenbaum
Chabad House
2014 Orrington
Evanston, IL 60201
312-869-8060

Rabbi Y. Schanowitz
North Suburban
Lubavitch Chabad
1871 Sheahen Court
Highland Park, IL 60035
312-433-1567

Rabbi Y. Posner
Lubavitch Chabad
of Skokie
4059 Dempster
Skokie, IL 60076
312-677-1770

Rabbi Y. Wolfe
Chabad Educational Center
5201 W. Howard
Skokie, IL 60077
312-675-6777

Indiana

Chabad House
518 East 7th Street
Bloomington, IN 47401
812-332-4511

Rabbi A. Grossbaum
1037 Golf Lane
Chabad House
Indianapolis, IN 46260
317-251-5573

Iowa

Rabbi M. Schanowitz
Chabad of Iowa
2932 University Avenue
Des Moines, IA 50311
515-279-7727

Kentucky

Chabad of Kentucky
333 Waller Avenue
Lexington, KY 40205
606-231-0320

Rabbi A. Litvin
Chabad House
Regional Headquarters
2607 Landor Avenue
Louisville, KY 40205
502-459-1770

Louisiana

Rabbi Z. Rivkin
Chabad of Louisiana
7037 Freret Street
New Orleans, LA 70118
504-866-5164

Maine

Rabbi M. Wilansky
Chabad Lubavitch
108 Noyes Street
Portland, ME 04103
207-871-8947

Maryland

Rabbi S. Kaplan
Bais Lubavitch
3505 Pinkney Road
Baltimore, MD 21215
301-358-1470

Rabbi H. Baron
Lubavitch Center
9650 Santiago Road #11
Columbia, MD 21045
301-740-2424

*Chabad-Lubavitch
Center; Miami Beach,
Florida, U.S.A.*

120

Rabbi B. Geisinsky
Chabad House
311 W. Montgomery Ave.
Rockville, MD 20850
301-340-6858

Massachusetts

Rabbi C. Adelman
Chabad House
30 N. Hadley Road
Amherst, MA 01002
413-549-4094

Rabbi C. Prus
Chabad House
491 Commonwealth Ave.
Boston, MA 02215
617-424-1190

Rabbi C. Ciment
Lubavitz Yeshiva
9 Prescott Street
Brookline, MA 02146
617-731-5330

Rabbi Y. Lazaros
Chabad House
of Framingham
74 Joseph Road
Framingham, MA 01701
617-877-8888

Rabbi A. Buklet
Chabad Center
9 Burlington Street
Lexington, MA 02173
617-863-8656

Rabbi D. Edelman
Yeshiva Achei Tmimim
1148 Converse Street
Longmeadow, MA 01106
413-567-8665

Rabbi M. Gurkov
Shaloh House
68 Smith Road
Milton, MA 02186
617-333-0477

Rabbi L. Fogelman
Chabad House Metro West
68 Heartford Street
Natick, MA 01760
508-651-9778

Chabad House
21 Elwood
Springfield, MA 01108
413-736-3936

Rabbi M. Gurkov
Shaloh House
50 Etyel Way
Stoughton, MA
617-344-6334

Rabbi H. Fogelman
Chabad Lubavitch
of Worcester
24 Creswell Road
Worcester, MA 01602
617-752-5791

Michigan

Rabbi A. Goldstein
Chabad House
715 Hill Street
Ann Arbor, MI 48104
313-769-3078

Rabbi C. Bergstein
Chabad House
of Farmington Hills
32000 Middlebelt Road
Farmington Hills, MI 48018
313-626-3194

Rabbi B. Shemtov
Lubavitch Foundation
28555 Middlebelt Road
Farmington Hills, MI 48018
313-737-7000

Rabbi Y. Weingarten
Chabad House
of Eastern Michigan
5394 Oaktree Drive
Flint, MI 48532
313-733-3779

Rabbi Y. Weingarten
Chabad House
of Western Michigan
2615 Michigan N.E.
Grand Rapids, MI 49506
616-957-0770

Rabbi Y. Kagan
Lubavitch Center
14000 W. 9 Mile Road
Oak Park, MI 48237
313-398-1888

Rabbi E. Silberberg
Chabad Torah Center
of West Bloomfield
5595 W. Maple Road
West Bloomfield, MI 48033
313-855-6170

Rabbi B. Stein
Cheder Oholei Yosef
Yitschak Lubavitch
14100 W. 9 Mile Road
Oak Park, MI 48237
313-541-5441

Minnesota

Rabbi D. Greene
Chabad House
730 2nd Street
Rochester, MN 55902
507-288-7500

Rabbi M. Feller
Lubavitch House
15 Montcalm Court
Saint Paul, MN 55116
612-698-3858

Missouri

Rabbi S. Wineberg
Chabad of Kansas City
8901 Holmes Street
Kansas City, MO 64131
816-333-7117

Rabbi Y. Landa
Chabad House of St. Louis
9648 Old Bonhomme Road
St. Louis, MO 63132
314-993-4630

Nebraska

Rabbi M. Katzman
Lubavitch of Omaha
640 S. 124th Avenue
Omaha, NE 68154
402-330-7400

New Hampshire

Rabbi L. Krinsky
Manchester, New Hampshire

New Jersey

Chabad Lubavitch
P.O. Box 304
Deal, NJ 07723
201-774-1358

Rabbi Z. Liberov
Chabad House
527 Grove Avenue
Edison, NJ 08820

Rabbi M. Kanelsky
Cong Ohel Yosef
Yitzchok-Bris Avrohom
555 Westminster Ave.
Elizabeth, NJ 07208
201-289-0770

Rabbi M. Kanelsky
Bris Avrohom
35 Cottage Street
Jersey City, NJ 07306
201-798-0056

Lubavitch of
Mercer County
701 White Pine Circle
Lawrenceville, NJ 08648
609-530-1373

Rabbi B. Chazanow
Chabad Lubavitch
of Western
Manmouth County
89 Old Queens Blvd.
Manalapan, NJ 07726
201-446-2701

Rabbi S. Rapoport
Lubavitch of
Atlantic County
8223 Fulton Avenue
Margate, NJ 08402
609-823-3223

Rabbi M. Herson
Rabbinical College of
America—Lubavitch
226 Sussex Avenue
Morristown, NJ 07960
201-267-9404

Rabbi J. Carlebach
Chabad House
8 Sicard Street
New Brunswick, NJ 08901
201-828-7374

Rabbi A. Herson
Chabad Center of
White Meadow Lake
23 Pawnee Avenue
Rockaway, NJ 07866
201-625-1525

Rabbi M. Weiss
Friends of Lubavitch
513 Kenwood Place
Teaneck, NJ 07666
201-568-9423

New York

Chabad House on Campus
One Commerce Plaza
Suite 806
Albany, NY 12260
518-465-8801

Rabbi Y. Rubin
Chabad of the
Capital District
122 S. Main Ave.
Albany, NY 13903
518-797-0015

Rabbi A. Slonim
Chabad Lubavitch
of Binghamton
1004 Murray Hill Road
Binghamton, NY 13903
607-797-0015

Rabbi H. Greenberg
Chabad House
3292 Main Street
Buffalo, NY 14216
716-837-2320

Knesset Center
500 Starin
Buffalo, NY 14216
716-832-5063

Lubavitch House
of Chautauqua
37 Miller Street
Chautauqua, NY 14722

Rabbi T. Teldon
Lubavitch of East L.I.
74 Hauppauge Rd.
Commack, NY 11725
516-462-6640

Rabbi L. Baumgarten
Lubavitch of The East End
6 Hyde Lane
Coram, NY 11727
516-732-1676

Rabbi N. Simon
Chabad House
of Delmar
109 Elsemere Avenue
Delmar, NY 12054
518-439-8280

Rabbi S. Zalmanow
Chabad House
of Flushing New York
150-02 78th Road
Flushing, NY 11367
718-380-7422

Rabbi N. Gurary
Chabad House
2501 N. Forest Road
Getzville, NY 14068
716-688-1642

Rabbi Y. Geisinsky
Great Neck, NY
718-953-6472

Chabad House
67 Fuller Road
Guilderlano, NY 12203
518-438-4227

*Chabad House;
Hartford, Connecticut,
U.S.A.*

Rabbi E. Zilberstein
Chabad House
902 Triphammer Road
Ithaca, NY 14850
607-257-7379

Rabbi A. Kotlarsky
Chabad Lubavitch
of Rockland
216 Congers Road
New City, NY 10956
914-634-0951

Rabbi E. Cohen
Chabad at New York
University
c/o JCF Rm. 715,
566 La Guardia
New York, NY 10012
212-727-1720

Rabbi S. Kugel
Chabad House of Upper
West Side
310 West 103rd Street
New York, NY 10025
212-864-5010

Rabbi Y. Borenstien
Chabad of Mid-Huddson
Valley
22 Lown Court
Poughkeepsie, NY 12603
914-454-1816

Rabbi N. Vogel
Chabad Lubavitch
36 Lattimore Road
Rochester, NY 14620
716-244-4324

Rabbi E. Benammau
Chabad of Saratoga
Pinewood Avenue
Saratoga, NY 12866

Rabbi Y. Friedman
Starrett City, NY
718-953-3764

Rabbi M. Katzman
Toras Emes Synagogue
3151 Hylan Blvd.
Staten Island, NY 10306
718-667-7844

Rabbi C. Grossbaum
Chabad House
of Stonybrook
2 Kenswick Drive
Stonybrook, NY 11790
516-689-2398

Rabbi Y. Rapoport
Chabad Lubavitch
113 Berkely Drive
Syracuse, NY 13210
315-424-0363

Rabbi L. Morrison
Troy Chabad Center
2306 15th Street
Troy, NY 12180
318-274-6562

Rabbi R. Flamer
Lubavitch of Westchester
5 Albermarle Road
White Plains, NY 10605
914-686-0725

Rabbi Y. Taubenfliegel
Chabad of the Catskills
P.O. Box 473
Woodridge, NY 12789
914-434-8570

North Carolina

Rabbi Y. Groner
Chabad House
921 Jefferson Road
Charlotte, NC 28226
704-366-3984

Ohio

Rabbi S. Kalmanson
Chabad House
1636 Summit Road
Cincinnati, OH 45237
513-821-5100

Rabbi L. Alevsky
Chabad House
2004 S. Green Road
Cleveland, OH 44121
216-382-5050

Chabad on Campus
3392 Desota Avenue
Cleveland, OH 44118
216-371-3679

Rabbi S. Kazen
Congregation
Tzemach Tzedek
1922 Lee Road
Cleveland Heights,
OH 44118
216-321-5169

Rabbi C. Capland
Chabad House
of Tradition
57 East 14th Avenue
Columbus, OH 43201
416-239-0124

Rabbi Y. Shemtov
Chabad House Lubavitch
of Toledo
2350 Secor Road
Toledo, OH 43606
419-535-1930

Oklahoma

Rabbi Y. Weg
Chabad House
6644 S. Victor Avenue
Tulsa, OK 74136
918-493-7006

Oregon

Rabbi M. Wilhelm
Chabad Center
14355 S.W. Scholls
Ferry Road
Beaverton, OR 97007
503-644-2997

Pennsylvania

Rabbi S. Pewzner
Chabad Lubavitch
3029 N. Front Street
Harrisburg, PA 17110
717-238-3638

Rabbi T. Perelman
Chabad House
102 3rd Avenue
Kingston, PA 18704
717-287-6336

Rabbi A. Shemtov
Lubavitch Center
7622 Castor Avenue
Philadelphia, PA 19152
215-725-2030

Rabbi M. Schmidt
Lubavitch House
754 S. 9th Street
Philadelphia, PA 19147
215-574-9280

Rabbi D. Kudan
Lubavitch House
4032 Spruce Street
Philadelphia, PA 19104
215-222-3130

Rabbi Z. Lipsker
Va'adah L'Dovrei
Ivrit Chabad
Castor Cor. Napfle
Philadelphia, PA 19152
215-725-2333

Rabbi S. Weinstein
Chabad House
4710 Wallingford Street
Pittsburgh, PA 15213
412-693-7770

Rabbi Y. Rosenfeld
Lubavitch Center
2100 Wightman Street
Pittsburgh, PA 15217
412-422-7300

Lubavitch Yeshiva Girls
2100 Wightman Street
Pittsburgh, PA 15217
412-422-7779

Rabbi S. Posner
Lubavitch Yeshiva
2410 Fifth Avenue
Pittsburgh, PA 15213
412-681-2446

Rhode Island

Rabbi Y. Laufer
Chabad House
Jewish Heritage
360 Hope Street
Providence, RI 02906
401-273-7238

South Carolina

Rabbi H. Epstein
Chabad House
6338 Goldbranch Road
Columbia, SC 29206
803-782-1831

Rabbi D. Aizenman
Chabad House
of Myrtle Beach
2803 North Oak Street
Myrtle Beach, SC 29577
803-448-0035

Tennessee

Rabbi Z. Posner
Congregation
Sherith Israel
3730 Whitland Avenue
Nashville, TN 37205
615-292-6614

Texas

Rabbi Y. Levertov
Chabad House
2101 Nueces Street
Austin, TX 78705
512-472-3900

Rabbi M. Dubrawsky
Chabad House
7008 Forest Lane
Dallas, TX 75230
214-361-8600

Rabbi I. Greenberg
Chabad House
6505 Westwind Drive
El Paso, TX 79912
915-833-5711

Rabbi M. Traxler
Chabad House at T.M.C.
1955 University Blvd.
Houston, TX 77030
713-522-2004

Rabbi S. Lazaroff
Chabad Lubavitch Center
10900 Fondren Road
Houston, TX 77096
713-777-2000

Rabbi C. Block
Chabad House
14535 Blanco Road
San Antonio, TX 78216
512-493-6503

Vermont

Rabbi Y. Raskin
Chabad House
230 College Street
Burlington, VT 05401
802-865-2770

Virginia

Rabbi Y. Bula
Chabad Lubavitch
of North Virginia
3924 Persimmon Drive
Fairfax, VA 22031
703-323-0233

Rabbi M. Gurkov
Chabad Lubavitch
of the Peninsula
425 Winterhaven Drive
Newport News, VA 23606
804-930-0302

Rabbi Y. Kranz
Lubavitch Center
of the Virginias
212 Gaskins Road
Richmond, VA 23233
804-740-2000

Rabbi A. Margolin
Chabad Lubavitch
of Tidewater
420 Investors Place, #102
Virginia Beach, VA 23452
804-490-9699

*Chabad-Lubavitch
Center;
Houston, Texas,
U.S.A.*

Chabad-Lubavitch School; Main Building; Johannesburg, South Africa.

Washington

Rabbi S. Levitin
Chabad House
4541 19th Avenue, N.E.
Seattle, WA 98105
206-527-1411

Wisconsin

Rabbi Y. Matusof
Chabad House
1722 Regent Street
Madison, WI 53705
608-231-3450

Rabbi Y. Shmotkin
Lubavitch House
3109 North Lake Drive
Milwaukee, WI 53211
414-962-0566

Rabbi D. Rapaport
Chabad House
2233 West Mequan Road
Mequan, WI 53092
414-242-2235

Argentina

Rabbi M. Birman
Beit Jabad Villa Crespo
Serrano 69
Buenos Aires, Argentina
1-855-9822

Rabbi M. Friedman
Beit Jabad
O'Higgins 584
Bahia Blanca, Argentina
91-22398

Rabbi S. Kiesel
Beit Jabad Belgrano
11 de Septiembre 858
Buenos Aires 1426,
Argentina

Rabbi N. Grunblatt
Beit Jabad Central
Jean Jaures 361
Buenos Aires 1215,
Argentina
1-875933

Rabbi T. Grunblatt
Chabad Lubavitch
Argentina Central
Aguero 1164
Buenos Aires, Argentina

Rabbi I. Kapelushnik
Beit Jabad Concordia
Uruguay 44
Concordia Entre Rios 3200
Argentina
45-217898

Rabbi E. Hazan
Beit Jabad Lanus
Antale France 1561 1-10
Prov. Buenos Aires 1824
Argentina,
1-241-0551

Rabbi S. Tawil
Beit Jabad Rosario
Rioja 1449 5A
Rosario 2000, Argentina
41-64845

Rabbi D. Levy
Beit Jabad Tucuman
Lamadrid 752
Tucuman 4000, Argentina
81-311257

Australia

Mr. K. Thomas
Chabad House
of Queensland
43 Cedar Street
Brisbane, Queensland
Australia
7-848-5886

Rabbi S. Jurkowicz
Chabad of Malvern
316 Glenferrie Road
Malvern 3144
Melbourne, Vic.
Australia
3-204-985

Rabbi Y. Gordon
Chabad House
of Tasmania
5 Brisbane Street
Tasmania, Australia
3-340705

Rabbi Y. Ulman
Chabad House
of North Bondi
25 O'Brien Street
N. Bondi, Sydney
NSW 2026, Australia
2-307752

Rabbi Y. Engel
Chabad House of St. Ives
23 Yarrabung Rd. St. Ives
Sydney NSW 2075,
Australia

Rabbi B. Lesches
Yeshivah Gedolah
Rabbinical College
24-36 Flood St., Bondi,
Sydney NSW 2026,
Australia
2-387-3822

Rabbi P. Woolstone
Jewish House
17 Flood St., Bondi
Sydney NSW 2026,
Australia
2-389-0311

Rabbi P. Feldman
Yeshiva Centre
24-36 Flood St., Bondi
Sydney NSW 2026,
Australia
2-387-3822

Rabbi E. Gorelik
Chabad House
for Russian Immigrants
366 Carlisle Street
Balaclava, Melbourne
Vic 3183, Australia
3-527-6234

Rabbi M. Raskin
Chabad of East Bentleigh
13-17 Cecil St. E.,
Bentleigh, Melbourne,
Vic 3165, Australia
3-579-0606

Rabbi A. Serebryanski
Merkos L'Inyonei Chinuch
118 Hotham St. E.,
St. Kilda, Melbourne,
Vic 3183, Australia

Rabbi S. Gurewicz
Bais Rivka Ladies College
14-20 Balaclava Rd. E.,
St. Kilda, Melbourne,
Vic 3183, Australia

Rabbi M. Shusterman
Ohel Chana
88 Hotham St.
East St. Kilda
Melbourne, Vic. 3183,
Australia
3-527-5461

Rabbi Y. Groner
Yeshiva Centre
92 Hotham St.
East St. Kilda
Melbourne, Vic. 3183,
Australia
3-527-4117/3768

Jewish Center
82 Hotham St.
East St. Kilda
Melbourne, Vic. 3183,
Australia

Rabbi B. Cohen
Yeshiva Gedolah
67 Alexandra St.
E. S. Kilda
Melbourne, Vic. 3183,
Australia
3-525-9165
3-527-6733

Rabbi P. Landes
Chabad of Perth
396 Alexander Drive
Noranda 6062
Western Australia
9-275-4912

Austria

Rabbi M. Israelov
Chabad House 2nd District
Serdinand Strasse #24
Vienna, Austria

Rabbi Y. Biderman
Chabad of Austria
Grunentorgasse #26
Vienna 1090, Austria
1-311149

Belgium

Rabbi S. Slavaticki
Chabad House
Brialmontlei 48
Antwerp 2000, Belgium
3-187-867

Rabbi S. Lasker
Beit Chabad
166 Ave. Adolf Buyl
Brussels, Belgium

Rabbi A. Chaikin
Lubavitch
Ave. Duroi 87
Brussels, 1060, Belgium
2-345-0522

Brazil

Rabbi D. Zagury
Beit Chabad do Brasil
Av Serezedeto
Correra 276
Belem 66040, Brazil
91-225-1994

Rabbi N. Katri
Beit Chabad do Brasil
Rua Timbrias 260/101
Belo Horizonte 30140
Brazil
31-225-2010

Rabbi J. Simonowits
Beit Chabad do Brasil
San 203 Bl. B/602
Brasilia 70233, DF Brazil
61-224-1561

Rabbi Y. Dubrawski
Beit Chabad do Brasil
Rua Vicente Machado 1222
Curitiba 80420, PR Brazil
41-224-5738

Rabbi Chaim Benjamini
Yeshiva Colegial
Machne Israel
C.P. 90372
Petropolis, RJ 25600 Brazil
242-42-4952

Rabbi M. Liberow
Beit Chabad do Brasil
R. Sta. Cecilia 1918
Porte Alegre 90410, Brazil
512-21-8765

Rabbi Y. Chazan
Beit Chabad do Brasil
Rua Dhalia 95
Recipe 51020, Brazil
81-325-1475

Rabbi Y. Goldman
Beit Lubavitch
R. Bom Pastor 514/302
Rio de Janeiro 20521 RJ,
Brazil
21-234-6782

Rabbi S. Alpern
Beit Chabad do Brasil
Headquarters
Rua Chabad 60
S. Paulo 01417, Brazil
11-282-8711, 282-0235

Rabbi Leibel Zajac
Tzeirei Agudas Chabad
R. Pde. Joao Manuel 758/11
S. Paulo 01411, Brazil
11-853-3376

Rabbi H. L. Begun
Instituto de
Ensino Lubavitch
R. Correa dos Santos 241
S. Paulo, 01124 SP, Brazil
11-220-3251

Rabbi Jacob Begun
Centro Tiferet
Lubavitch
R. Alagoas 725
S. Paulo 01239 SP, Brazil
11-66-7783

Rabbi Yossi Schildkraut
Beit Chabad do Brazil
Rua Russia 195
S. Paulo (Itaim)
01448 SP, Brazil
11-282-0576

Rabbi S. Ende
Beit Chabad do Brasil
Rua Primerio
de Maio 126/22
S. Andre, Brazil
11-412-9625

Canada

Alberta

Rabbi M. M. Matusof
Lubavitch of Alberta
Calgary, Alberta

British Columbia

Rabbi M. Altein
Chabad House of Kitsilano
2819 West 5th Ave.
Vancouver, BC V6K 1T8,
Canada
604-731-7733

Rabbi Y. Wineberg
Lubavitch of British
Columbia
5750 Oak Street
Vancouver, BC V6M 2V7,
Canada
604-266-1313

Manitoba

Rabbi A. Altein
Chabad House
2095 Sinclair
Winnipeg, Manitoba
R2V 3K2, Canada
204-339-8737

Nova Scotia

Atlantic Jewish County
1515 S. Park St., #304
Halifax, Nova Scotia
B3J 2L2, Canada
902-422-7491

Ontario

Cong Beth Joseph
44 Edinburgh Drive
Downsview, Ontario
M3H 4B1, Canada
416-633-0380

Rabbi Z. Itkin
Chabad Lubavitch
Hamilton
87 Westwood Ave.
Hamilton, Ontario
L8S 2B1, Canada
416-529-7458

Rabbi Y. Block
Chabad House
216 Bernard Avenue
London, Ontario
N6A 2M8, Canada
519-673-0153

Rabbi A. Plotkin
Chabad Lubavitch
Markham
135 Holm Crescent
Markham, Ontario
L3T 5J4, Canada
416-881-0154

Rabbi P. Sperlin
Chabad House
64 Templeton Street
Ottawa, Ontario
K1N 6X3, Canada
613-234-6214

Rabbi Z. Grossbaum
Chabad Lubavitch
Community Center
770 Chabad Gate
Thornhill, Ontario
L4J 3V9, Canada
416-731-7000

Rabbi J. Zaltzman
Jewish Russian
Community Center
18 Rockford Road
Willowdale, Ontario
M2R 3V9, Canada
416-633-9333

Quebec

Rabbi M. New
Chabad House
of Chomedy
848 Connaught Circle
Chomedy, Quebec
H7W 1N9, Canada
514-687-2709

Rabbi M. Raskin
Chabad House of C.S.L.
7101 Cote S. Luc Road
Cote St. Luc, Quebec
H4V 1G2, Canada
514-485-7221

Rabbi N. Perlstein
Chabad High
7500 Mackle Road
Cote St. Luc, Quebec
H4W 1A6, Canada
514-842-6616

Bais Rivkah Academy
5001 Vezina St.
Montreal, Quebec
H3W 1C2, Canada
514-731-3681

Rabbi S. Chriqui
Centre Chabad
4691 Van Horne
Montreal, Quebec
H3W 1H3, Canada
514-738-4654

Rabbi R. Fine
Chabad House
3429 Peel Street
Montreal, Quebec
H3A 1W7, Canada
514-842-6616

Rabbi B. Mockin
Chabad Lubavitch Youth
Organization
3429 Peel Street
Montreal, Quebec
H3A 1W7, Canada
514-842-6616

Rabbi Y. Sirota
Chabad Russian Center
5181 Bourret Ave.
Montreal, Quebec
Canada
514-737-5438

Rabbinical College
of Canada T.T.L.
6405 Westbury Avenue
Montreal, Quebec
H3W 2X5, Canada

Rabbi Y. Paris
Free Hebrew Schools
for Juniors-Lubavitch
4649 Van Horne #2D
Montreal, Quebec
H3W-1H8, Canada
514-735-2255

Chile

Rabbi M. Perman
Jabad Lubavitch de Chile
Eliodoro Yanez 2980
Santiago de Chile, Chile
2-231-8711

Colombia

Rabbi M. Zaifrani
Casa Lubavitch
Carera #56 75-20
Baranquilla, Colombia

Rabbi Y. Rosenfeld
Casa Lubavitch
Calle 94 #11-47
Bogota, Colombia
1-236-3114

England

Rabbi S. Arkush
Lubavitch House
95 Willows Road
Birmingham B12 9QB,
England
21-440-6673

Chabad House
Bournemouth
8 Gordon Road, Boscome,
Bournemouth, Dorset
BH1 4DW, England

Chabad House
42 Welbeck Street
East London, W1, England
1-935-7242

Rabbi L. Sudak
Chabad House
232 Hale Lane
Edgware, Middlesex
HA8 8SR, England
1-958-8417

Rabbi P. Efune
Chabad House-Brighton
15 The Upper Drive
Hove, East Sussex
BN3 6OR, England
273-21219

Rabbi A. Sufrin
Chabad Lubavitch
Community Center
372 Cranbrook Road
Ilford, Essex 162 6HW,
England
1-554-1624

Rabbi Y. Angyalfi
Lubavitch Leisure
and Cultural Center
168 Shadwell Lane
Leeds, LS178AD, England
532-663311

Bais Chana
19 Northfield Road
London, N16 5RP, England
1-809-6508

Chabad House Hendon
3/4 Sentinel Square,
Brent Street
London NW4, England
1-202-1477

Rabbi N. Sudak
Lubavitch Foundation
U.K. Headquarters
107-115 Stamford Hill
London N16 5RP, England
1-800-0022

Rabbi Y. Herz
Yeshivah Gedolah
Lubavitch
3-5 Kingsley Way
London N20 EH, England
1-458-2312

Rabbi G. Overlander
Chabad House
75 Cowley Road
Oxford OX4 1HD,
England
865-782-462

Lubavitch House
Manchester
62 Singleton Road
Salford, Lancs M7 OLU,
England
61-740-9514

Rabbi N. Dubov
Chabad House
6 Pine Grove
Wimbledon,
London SW19, England
1-946-3445

France

Rabbi A. Geribi
Beit Habad
19 Ave. Victor Hugo
Aix en Provience 13100
France
42-38-69-21

Rabbi M. Deutsh
Beth Habad
D'Aubervilliers
150-154 Rue Andre
Karman, Aubervilliers
93300, France
1-43-52-78-49

Beth Loubavitch
8 Rue Partleur
Bonneuil, France
1-43-77-07-63

*Chabad-Lubavitch
Central Office;
Buenos Aires,
Argentina.*

Rabbi Y. Nemanow
Yeshivas Tomchei Tmimim
Yeshiva Gedola
2 Bis Avenue du Petit
Chateau, Brundy 91800,
France
1-60-46-31-46

Rabbi Y. Cohen
Beth Habad
15 Bal D'Alsace
Cannes 06400, France
92-48-91-98

Beth Loubavitch
28 Ave. de Newburn
Choisy-Orly 94600
France
1-48-53-48-27

Beth Loubavitch
Rue 8 Mai 1945
Creteil, France
1-43-39-20-05

Beth Loubavitch
3 Rue Jean Zay
Fontenay Sous Bois 94120,
France
1-48-73-92-59

Rabbi Y. Lahiany
Beit Habad
10 Rue Lazare Carnot
Grenoble 38000, France
76-43-29-99

Rabbi E. Dahun
Beth Chabad
76 Boulevard de Metz
Lille 59000, France
20-54-22-74

Rabbi S. Gurewitz
Beth Habad
3 Passage Cazenove
Lyon 69006, France
78-89-08-32

Rabbi Y. Labkowski
Beth Habad
112 Bd Barry
Marseille 13013, France
91-06-00-61

Rabbi J. Pinson
Beth Habad
Menton, France
93-82-46-86

Rabbi Y. Matusof
Beth Habad
41 Rue du Rabbin E. Bloch
Metz 57000, France
87-36-09-24

Rabbi P. Partouche
Beth Habad
5 Rue Bayard
Montpellier 34000, France
67-64-59-65

Rabbi Y. Matusof
Bibliotheque Ouforatsto
19 Bd Joffre
Nancy 54000, France
87-36-80-88

Rabbi J. Pinson
Beth Lubavitch-Habad
22 Rue Rossini
Nice 06000, France
93-82-46-86

Beth Loubavitch
166 Rue Brossellet
Noisy (Le Grand), France
1-45-26-87-60

Rabbi H. Pevzner
Beis Habad
Sinai Loubavitch
37 Rue Pajol
Paris 75018, France
1-46-07-54-57

Beth Loubavitch
53 Rue Compans
Paris 75019, France
1-42-05-08-13

Rabbi C. Azimov
Beth Loubavitch
8 Rue Lamartine
Paris 75009, France
1-45-26-87-60

Beth Loubavitch
59/65 Rue de Flandre
Paris 75019, France
1-42-41-93-90

Beth Loubavitch
82 Rue Couronnes
Paris 75020, France
1-45-26-87-60

Beth Loubavitch
93 Rue Orteaux
Paris 75020, France
1-45-26-87-60

Beth Loubavitch
17 Rue de Rosiers
Paris 75004, France
1-45-26-87-60

Rabbi B. Gorodetzky
Bureau European
de Lubavitch
8 Rue Meslay
Paris 75003, France
1-48-87-87-12

Rabbi Y. Bitton
Beth Chabad Lubavitch
8 Place Jean Moulin
Sarcelles 95200, France
1-39-90-82-32

Rabbi S. Samama
Beth Habad Strasbourg
2 Rue de Niederbronn
Strasbourg 6700, France
88-36-75-39

Rabbi Y. Matusof
Jeunesse Lubavitch-
Beth Habad
8 Rue du Pont Montaudran
Toulouse 31000, France
61-62-46-84

Beth Loubavitch
154 Bis. Ave. Gallieni
Villeneuve La Garanne
92390, France
1-47-58-94-71

Beth Rivkah Seminary
45 Ave. Raymond Poincare
Yerres 91330, France
1-69-48-46-01

Holland

Rabbi B. Jacobs
Lubavitch
Operaweg 101
Amerssfoort 381-GEC,
Holland
33-726-204

Rabbi M. Vorst
Beis Chabad-Lubavitch
Havikhorst 85
Amstelveen-Amsterdam
Holland
20-466017

Lubavitch
Lorentzkade 222
Haarlem, Holland
23-242051

Lubavitch
Pieter Niew Landstr 71
Utrecht, Holland
30-732453

Hong Kong

Rabbi M. Avtzon
Chabad Lubavitch
of Hong Kong
27 MacDonnell Rd. #1B
Hong Kong, Hong Kong
5-239-770

Israel

Rabbi E. Wolf
Agudat Chasidei Chabad
P.O.B. 46
Lod 71100, Israel
8-224-392

Rabbi Y. Lebov
Rabbi Y. Aranov
Lubavitch Youth
Organization—
Central Office
P.O.B. 14 Beit Shazar
K'Far Chabad 72915, Israel
3-9607588

Rabbi N. Oierchman
Chabad of Acre
15 Ben Ami St., P.O.B. 2564
Acre 24124, Israel
4-918633

Rabbi M. Mohal
Chabad of Aderet
Doar Na Haela
Aderet, Israel
3-960-6077

Rabbi C. Segal
Chabad of Afula
2 Kikar Ha'Atzmaut
P.O.B. 26, Afula 18100,
Israel
65-92339

Rabbi Y. Rubin
Chabad of Alon Moreh
Doar Na Lev Hashomron
Alon Moreh, Israel
53-72405

Rabbi I. Raskin
Chabad of Arad
37 Chen Street #3
Arad 80700, Israel
57-953330

Rabbi S. Omer
Chabad of Ariel
4/13 Ashdar St., P.O.B. 667
Ariel 90920, Israel
52-921084

Rabbi S. Goodman
Chabad of Ashdod
671 Kibbutz Galuyot St.,
P.O.B. 2034
Ashdod 77120, Israel
8-533511

Rabbi M. Laufer
4 Ruguzon Street
Building Panlon
Ashdod 77120, Israel
8-522556

Rabbi M. Lieberman
Chabad of Ashkelon
714 Shapira St. #22,
P.O.B. 7457
Ashkelon 78000, Israel
51-55668

Rabbi U. Cohen
6 Tzahal St., P.O.B. 136
Ashkelon 78000, Israel
51-28428

Rabbi M. Axelrod
Chabad of Atlit
P.O.B. 1520
Atlit 30350, Israel
4-841497

Rabbi Y. Yadgar
Chabad of Avital
Doar Na Yisrael
Avital Ta'Anach 19365,
Israel
6-591609

Rabbi D. Cohen
Chabad of Avivim
Avivim, Israel
6-972781

Rabbi S. Yardeny
Chabad of Azur
P.O.B. 70
Azur, Israel
3-556-1180

Chabad of B'Nei Braq
99 Rabbi Akivah St.
P.O.B. 269
B'Nai Braq, Israel
3-790885

Rabbi A. Shapira
Chabad of Pardes Katz-
B'Nei Braq
Abramsky 37
B'Nai Braq, Israel
3-579-0515

Rabbi S. Ma'Atuf
Chabad of Bareket
28 Bareket
Bareket 73185, Israel
3-972-1004

Rabbi Z. Tzik
Chabad of Bat Yam
67 Ha'Atzmaut Ave.,
Migdal Nachum,
P.O.B. 3084
Bat Yam 59130, Israel
3-860692

*Rebbetzin Chaya
Mushka Girls' School;
Los Angeles,
California, U.S.A.*

Rabbi S. Ushki
Chabad of Ramat Hanasi
26 Harav Maimon St.
P.O.B. 1222
Bat Yam 59620, Israel
3-552-1494

Rabbi A. Cohen
Chabad House
Rechavat Chatam Sofer,
Shchunah 11
Be'er Sheva 84000, Israel
57-431227

Rabbi T. Barashensky
Chabad of Be'er Sheva
88 Hachalutz St.
Be'er Sheva 84208, Israel
57-75244

Rabbi S. Grumach
Chabad of Beit Dagan
72 Ha'Atzmaut St.
Beit Dagan 50200, Israel
03-9606784

Rabbi Y. Shmulevitz
Chabad of Beit Sha'an
19 Shikun Chisachon #14
P.O.B. 493
Beit Sha'an 10900, Israel
6-588604

Rabbi E. Veiner
Chabad of Beit Shemesh
132 Hanarkis #9
Givat Sheret, P.O.B. 496
Beit Shemesh, Israel
02-913030

Rabbi M. Katz
Chabad of Ben Dor
5 Hatichon St.
Ben Dor 20306, Israel
4-239-044

Rabbi Y. Adot
Chabad of Binyamina
Hameyasdim St., P.O.B. 12
Binyamina, Israel
6-380006

Rabbi A. Bashari
Chabad of Biria
Biria, Israel
6-974070

Chabad of Brosh
Doar Na Hanegev
Brosh, Israel
57-923103

Rabbi Y. Rivkin
Chabad of Carmiel
Merkaz Hamischari,
P.O.B. 626
Carmiel 20101, Israel
4-988915

Rabbi K. Kupchik
Chabad of Chadera
45 Achad Ha'am St.
Chadera, Israel
6-337535

Rabbi Y. Gazit
Chabad of Chatzor Haglilit
730 Hageulim #6,
P.O.B. 5170
Chatzor Haglilit 10300,
Israel
6-934039

Rabbi Y. Gelis
Chabad of Dimona
60 Shdirot Hertzel #2
P.O.B. 772
Dimona 86107, Israel
57-51961

Rabbi M. Tamri
Chabad of Dishon
Doar Na Mevoot Chermon
Dishon, Israel
6-974113

Rabbi S. Levkivkar
Chabad of Dovav
Dovav, Israel
6-792764

Rabbi Y. Glitzenstein
Chabad of Eilat
P.O.B. 36
Eilat 88100
Israel
59-32363

Rabbi Pash
Chabad of
Kibbutz Ein Hanatziv
Ein Hanatziv 10805, Israel
6-582948

Rabbi B. Karneil
Chabad of G'Dera
11 Shprinsek St. P.O.B. 61
G'Dera 70700, Israel
8-596534

Rabbi S. Dahan
Chabad of Gan Yavneh
Miron St.
Schechunat Neve Zipora
Gan Yavneh 70800, Israel
8-584520

Rabbi B. Huss
Chabad of Ganei Tikvah
64 Harey Yehudah,
Givat Sevyon
Ganei Tikvah 70800, Israel
3-345-146

Rabbi G. Reuveni
Chabad of Gelulim
Geulim, Israel

Rabbi L. Schildkraut
Chabad of Haifa
37 Nordan St. P.O.B. 5348
Haifa 33211, Israel
4-643704

Rabbi Y. Halperin
Chabad of Hertzlia
37 Ha'Atzmaut St.
P.O.B. 5208
Hertzlia 46130, Israel
52-546146

Rabbi Y. Leider
Chabad of Cholon
82 Sokolov St.
Holon, Israel
3-849869

Rabbi E. Vogel
Chabad of Bait Vagan
7 Kasutu
Jerusalem, Israel
2-430547

Rabbi B. K'Limi
Chabad of Eir Ganim
P.O.B. 26268
117 Kostarika St. #20
Jerusalem 96625, Israel
2-411121

Rabbi A. Halperin
Chabad of French Hill
6 Hahagana St.
Jerusalem 97852, Israel
2-815196

Rabbi D. Dahan
Chabad of Giloh
Merkaz Mischari Chadash
800A
Jerusalem 91110, Israel
2-764623

Rabbi M. Stern
Chabad of
Givat Shaul-Har Nof
29 Kanfei Nesharim St.
Merkaz Sapir P.O.B. 1336
Jerusalem 91013, Israel
2-524098

Rabbi Y. Ralbag
Chabad of Kiryat Yovel
22 Uruguay St. P.O.B. 9334
Jerusalem 91092, Israel
2-411206

Rabbi S. Gamleal
Chabad of
Merkaz Yerushalayim
5 Uriel St. P.O.B. 5419
Jerusalem 97363, Israel
2-827224

Rabbi S. Pozilov
Chabad of Pisgat Zeev
22 Moshe Dayan St. #44
Jerusalem, Israel
2-858293

Rabbi R. Greenfeld
Chabad of Ramot
7 Shirat Hayam St.
Jerusalem 97725, Israel
2-858598

Chabad of
The Old City Jerusalem
31 Chabad St.
Jerusalem 97500, Israel
2-283135

Rabbi Y. Yusevitch
Yeshiva Gedola
Torat Emet Chabad
17 Chana St.
Jerusalem, Israel

Chabad Library
21 Y'Shayahu St. Geula
Jerusalem/Geulah
Israel

Rabbi S. Chefer
Beit Rivkah, Tichon
K'Far Chabad 72915
Israel
3-960 6571

Rabbi M. Friedman
Chabad of K'Far Chabad
P.O.B. 14
K'Far Chabad 72915
Israel
3-9607588

Rabbi A. Kanyevky
Chabad of K'Far Saba
128 Weizman St. P.O.B. 343
K'Far Saba 44102, Israel
52-26854

Rabbi Y. Hertzel
Chabad of K'Far Tavor
P.O.B. 63
K'Far Tavor 15241, Israel
6-767384

Rabbi C No'Am
Chabad of Kfar Yavetz
Doar Na Sharon Tichon
K'Far Yavetz 45830, Israel
52-63055

Rabbi Z. Friedman
Chabad of Kalanit
7 Kiryat Maor Chaim #61
Kalanit, Israel
6-931834

Rabbi M. Shalter
Chabad of Karnei Shomron
P.O.B. 185
Karnei Shomron 44853
Israel, 52-929164

Rabbi N. Schwartz
Chabad of Katzrin
5 Mishol Orcha St. #17
P.O.B. 3595
Katzrin 12900, Israel
6-962229

Rabbi B. Nachshon
Chabad of Kiryat Arba
P.O.B. 84
Kiryat Arba 90100, Israel
2-964897

Rabbi C. Diskin
Chabad of Kiryat Ata
14 Zevulun St. P.O.B. 5267
Kiryat Ata 28000
Israel, 4-453434

Rabbi S. Frumer
Chabad of Kiryat Bialik
43 Keren Hayisod St.
P.O.B. 5770
Kiryat Bialik 27157, Israel
4-716390

Rabbi S. Volpo
Chabad of Kiryat Gat
Shederot Lachish P.O.B. 280
Kiryat Gat 82102, Israel
51-882493

Rabbi L. Kurtzveil
Chabad of Kiryat Malahi
176 Nachlat Har Chabad
#19, Kirya Malahi 70900
Israel
8-583799

Rabbi M. Oirechman
Chabad of Kiryat Motzkin
46 Shderot Moshe Goshan
P.O.B. 770
Kiryat Motzkin 26310
Israel
4-719418

Chabad House;
Coral Springs, Florida,
U.S.A.

Rabbi C. Parsiko
Chabad of Kiryat Ono
Kiryat Ono, Israel
3-345253

Rabbi I. Tzipori
Chabad of Kiryat Shmona
P.O.B. 224, 308/6 Halvanon
Kiryat Shmona 10200, Israel
6-943-928

Rabbi M. Althoiz
Chabad of Kiryat Tivon
5 Hachoresh St. P.O.B. 1201
Kiryat Tivon 36111, Israel
4-936140

Chabad of Kiryat Yam
7 Shderot Weizman
P.O.B. 531
Kiryat Yam 29105, Israel
4-755792

Rabbi N. Maidantzik
Chabad of Ben Gurion
Airport-Lod
P.O.B. 218 Airport
Lod, Israel
3-971-0427

Rabbi Y. Gloiberman
Chabad of Lod
1 Kikar Ha'Atzmaut
P.O.B. 41
Lod 71100, Israel
8-240280

Rabbi A. Samla
Chabad of Ma'Ale Adomim
55 Hanecholim St. P.O.B. 26
Ma'Ale Adomim 90610
Israel
2-352402

Rabbi E. Asayag
Chabad of Ma'Alot
432 Zabotinski P.O.B. 2207
Ma'Alot 24952, Israel
4-978275

Rabbi A. Donin
Chabad of Maitav
Ta'Anach Hamizrachit
Maitav-Ta'Anach 19369
Israel
6-591340

Rabbi B. Kohen
Chabad of Mavo Modi'In
Doar Na Mavo Modi'In
Mavo Modi'In 73122
Israel

Rabbi D. Vaknin
Chabad of Menachemya
6 Shuchnat Ofer
Menachemya 14945, Israel
6-751294

Rabbi A. Rabinowitz
Chabad of Mevaseret
Yerushalayim
113 Hashlom St. #3
P.O.B. 223
Mevaseret Yerushalayim
Israel
2-343210

Rabbi E. Prasia
Chabad of Midgal Ha'Emek
592 Ha'Atzmaut St. #1
P.O.B. 267
Migdal Ha'Emek 10552
Israel
6-541339

Rabbi I. Butman
Chabad of Naharia
16 Shderot Hagaaton
Naharia 22402, Israel
4-924875

Rabbi D. Nachshon
Chabad Mitzvah Tanks
KiKar Magen David
P.O.B. 1035
Natzeret Ilit 17110, Israel
6-374-266

Rabbi Y. Lipsker
Chabad of Nazeret Ilit
7 Charod St. #53
Natzeret Ilit 17000, Israel
6-572-470

Rabbi Y. Doch
Chabad of
Shchunat Tzfonit
134 Arbell St.
Natzeret Ilit, Israel
6-577-401

Rabbi R. Faigin
Chabad of Nes Tziyona
4 Rotshild St. P.O.B. 214
Nes Ziyona 76400, Israel
8-465624

Rabbi E. Turgman
Chabad of Azurim
17 Merkaz Mischary
P.O.B. 2073
Netanya 42120, Israel
53-52947

Rabbi M. Volpa
Chabad of Netanya
13 Semilansky St.
Netanya, Israel
53-333-037

Rabbi Y. Edrehee
Chabad of Netivot
P.O.B. 162
Netivot 80250, Israel
57-943219

Rabbi Y. Kirshnzaft
Chabad of Chevel Azah
Neve Dekalim, Israel
51-47210

Rabbi Y. Shtrasberg
Chabad of Neve Monson
Neve Monson, Israel
3-9606915

Rabbi Y. Burgan
Chabad of Nir Tzvi
Nir Tzvi, Israel
3-960 6896

Rabbi Y. Hershkovitz
Chabad of Ofakim
1448 Giborei Yisrael St.
P.O.B. 216
Ofakim 80351, Israel
57-926034

Rabbi E. Shmulevitz
Chabad of
Ohr Akivah-Kesaria
P.O.B. 143
Ohr Akivah-Kesaria 30600
Israel
6-360153

Rabbi T. Bolton
Chabad of Ohr Yehudah
32 David Elazar St.
Ohr Yehuda, Israel
3-712226

Rabbi Y. Ginzburg
Chabad of Omer
P.O.B. 117
Omer 84965, Israel
57-690903

Rabbi Y. Kurant
Chabad of Pardes Chana
63 Derech Pika
Pardes Chana 37000
Israel
6-378057

Rabbi M. Rabinowitz
Chabad of Petach Tikva
88 Rotchild St. P.O.B. 720
Petah Tiqwa 49612, Israel
3-9227134

Rabbi E. Shadmi
Chabad of Ra'Anana
6 Borochov St.
Ra'Anana 43251, Israel
52-26744

Rabbi C. Tzadok
Chabad of Ramat Amidar
2 Olei Hagardom St.
Ramat Gan, Israel
3-5741158

Rabbi M. Gal
Chabad of Ramat Gan
18 Bailick St. P.O.B. 10893
Ramat Gan, Israel
3-737910

Rabbi Y. Volosov
Chabad of Ramat Yishai
Ramat Yishai, Israel
4-835647

Rabbi C. Topol
Chabad of Ramla
56-57 Merkaz Mischari
Ramla, Israel
8-243777

Rabbi M. Shaer
Chabad of Kiryat Moshe
10 Borochov St.
Rechovot 76406, Israel
8-451392

Rabbi A. Kastel
Chabad of Rechovot
155 Hertzel St. P.O.B. 1118
Rechovot 76110, Israel
8-456817

Rabbi Y. Gruzman
Chabad of Rishon L'Tzion
44 Hertzel St.
P.O.B. 3195-75100
Rishon L'Tzion 75268
Israel
3-9643482

Rabbi B. Akivah
Chabad of Rosh Ha'Ayin
8 Chazon Eish St. P.O.B. 278
Rosh Ha'Ayin 40860, Israel
3-9369769

Rabbi S. Berkowitz
Chabad of Rosh Pina
24 Hachalutzim St.
P.O.B. 110
Rosh Pinah 12000, Israel
6-953360

Rabbi G. Marzel
Chabad of Old City
28 Chatam Sofer St.
Safed 13203, Israel
6-931414

Rabbi A. Kaplan
Chabad of Safed
P.O. Box 374
Safed, Israel

Rabbi S. Bloch
Chabad of
Shechunat Cna'An
Safed, Israel
6-973644

Rabbi Y. Lipsh
Chabad of
Shechunat Rasko
P.O.B 374
Safed 13102, Israel
6-974005

Rabbi S. Leiter
Machon Ascent
6 Ridbaz St. P.O.B. 296
Safed 13000, Israel
6-971407

Rabbi M. Mashash
Chabad of Safsufa
Doar Na Marom Hagalil
Safsufa 13875, Israel
6-980001

Rabbi Y. Cohen
Chabad of Savyon
Savyon, Israel

Rabbi Z. Pizem
Chabad of Sderot
90 Ron Shukron St.
P.O.B. 391
Sderot 80100, Israel
51-891707

Rabbi D. Notik
Chabad of Shefer
Shefer, Israel
6-971019

Rabbi R. Levinson
Chabad of Tel Adashim
Tel Adashim, Israel
6-526118

Chabad of Ramat Aviv
7 Hadaf Hayomi
Tel Aviv 17417, Israel
3-582458

Rabbi Y. Gerlitzky
Beit Chabad
University of Tel Aviv
Tel Aviv, Israel

Rabbi Y. Gerlitzky
Chabad of Tel Aviv
13 Hadassah St.
Tel Aviv 61162, Israel
3-239252

Rabbi E. Tamam
Chabad of Jaffa
94 Jerusalem St.
Tel Aviv/Jaffa 68180, Israel
3-832730

Rabbi M. Kurant
Chabad of Nesher
P.O.B. 466, 9 Barak St. #3
Tel Chanan, Israel
4-231683

Rabbi A. Shaatel
Chabad of Tel Mond
Tel Mond, Israel
52-63335

Rabbi Y. Kramer
Chabad of Tiberias
Haprachim St. P.O.B. 403
Tiberias 14130, Israel
6-732030

Rabbi Y. Markovitz
Chabad of Tirat Hakarmel
Hamerkaz Hamischari
P.O.B. 224
Tirat Hakarmel 30252,
Israel
4-574157

Rabbi S. Taizi
Chabad of Tirat Yehuda
Tirat Yehuda, Israel
8-228196

Rabbi Y. Lasker
Chabad of Yahud
9 Tzvi Yishay P.O.B. 216
Yahud 56267, Israel
3-960 7051

Rabbi Y. Lerer
Chabad of Yavneh
10 Shderot Duani #1
P.O.B. 420
Yavneh 70600, Israel
8-435797

Rabbi Y. Raitzis
Chabad of Yesod Hama'Ala
Yesod Hama'Ala, Israel
6-937601

Rabbi N. Dekel
Chabad of Yokne'Am Elite
2 Ha'Alonim St. #3
P.O.B. 4227
Yonkneam Eilite 20692
4-890021

Rabbi Y. Katz
Chabad Zichron Yaakov
P.O.B. 290
Zichron Yaakov 30952
Israel
6-398-686

Italy

Rabbi E. Borenstein
Bais Chabad
Via Dagnini 24
Bologna 40137, Italy
51-340936

Rabbi T. Rabisky
Beis Chabad-
Persian Center
Via Fiume
Ladispoli 00055, Italy
6-992-6447

Rabbi T. Rabisky
Beis Chabad-
Russian Center
Via Genova 26
Ladispoli 00055, Italy
6-992-6447

Bais Chabad
Via F. Bronzetti 18
Milan 20129, Italy

Rabbi G. Garelik
Merkos L'Inyonei Chinuch
Via C. Poerio 35
Milan 20129, Italy

Tzach
Via Le Piceno 23/A
Milan 20129, Italy
2-7610531

Rabbi Y. Hazan
Bais Chabad of Rome
Via Ottavio Panciroli 7
Rome 00162, Italy
6-424-6962

Mexico

Campeche 255
Mexico City, 7
Mexico
5-742224

Fuente De Ceres 7,
Tecamachio
Mexico City, 5 DF
Mexico
5-890656

Morocco

Rabbi S. Eidelman
Kollel Avrchim Lubavitch
Neve Shalom
27 Rue Verlet Hanus
Casablanca, Morocco
27-45-10

Rabbi S. Matusof
Oholei Yossef Yitzchok
Lubavitch
174 Blvd. Zira 001
Casablanca, Morocco
27-91-95

Rabbi Y. Raskin
Juenesse Uforatzta
Lubavitch
10 Rue Washington
Casablanca, Morocco
26-90-37

Paraguay

Rabbi Y. Forma
Beit Chabad de Paraguay
Calle Paraguari 771
Assuncion, Paraguay
21-95-441

Peru

Rabbi S. Z. Blumenfeld
Chabad Lubavitch de Peru
Aureio Miro Quesada
270/202
Lima, Peru
14-416-261

Romania

Chabad Lubavitch
Bucharest, Romania
400-150-572

Scotland

Rabbi C. Jacobs
Lubavitch Foundation
of Scotland
8 Orchard Drive
Giffnock,
Glasgow G46 7NR
Scotland
41-638-6116

South Africa

Rabbi M. Lipskar
Lubavitch Foundation
of Southern Africa
57 Oaklands Rd. Orchards
Johannesburg 2192
South Africa
11-640-7561

Rabbi M. Popack
Chabad Centre
6 Holmfirth Rd., Seapoint
Cape Town 8001
South Africa
21-443740

Chabad House
of Johannesburg
33 Harley St., Yeoville
Johannesburg 2198
South Africa
11-648-1133

Rabbi Hecht
Chabad House of Sandton
Chabad Place
P.O.B. 7861 Gallo Manor,
Sandton
Johannesburg 2052
South Africa
11-648-1133

Rabbi A. Katz
Chabad of Illovo
49 4th Ave.
Johannesburg
South Africa

Rabbi A. Carlebach
Chabad of Lyndhurst
147 Morkel Rd., Lyndhurst
Johannesburg 2192
South Africa
11-640-5100

Rabbi Y. Shusterman
Chabad of Victoria
17 Shipstone Lane
Victoria, Johannesburg 2192
South Africa
11-640-7593

Rabbi L. Wineberg
Lubavitch Yeshivah Gedolah
55 Oaklands Rd.
Johannesburg 2192
South Africa
11-640-7562

Rabbi D. Masinter
Chabad of the North Coast
Umhlanga Durban
South Africa

Spain

Rabbi Y. Goldstein
Bet Jabad
Calle Jordan 9 Apt 4D
Madrid 28010, Spain
1-445-9629

Switzerland

Rabbi M. Pewzner
Chabad Lubavitch
Geneva, Switzerland

Rabbi M. Rosenfeld
Beth Chabad
Manessestrasse 198
Zurich 8045, Switzerland
1-201-1691

Tunisia

Rabbi N. Pinson
Chabad Lubavitch
73 Rue de Palestine
Tunis, Tunisia
1-288-460

Uruguay

Rabbi E. Shemtov
Centro Lubavitch
Sarmiento 2644
Montevideo 70661
Uruguay
2-70-1457

Venezuela

Rabbi T. Lipinsky
Hogar Jabad Lubavitch
11A Avenida
Con 8A Trnsversal
Caracas 1062, Venezuela
2-261-9743

Rabbi L. Shochat
Yeshiva Gedola
of Venezuela
Av. Jorge Washington #8
Caracas, Venezuela
2-51-41-67

Rabbi M. Perman
Chabad Lubavitch
de Venezuela
Av. Eraso
Res. Bella Vista P.H.
San Bernardino, Caracas
Venezuela
2-52-38-87

West Germany

Rabbi Y. Diskind
Munich, West Germany

*Bet Rivkah Seminary
Campus; Paris, France.*

Chabad-Lubavitch Institutions Worldwide

Canada

United States

Panama

Venezuela

Colombia

Peru

Brazil

Paraguay

Argentina

Uruguay

Chile

Legend

☐ 1 center
☐ 2–10 centers
■ more than 10 centers

Chabad-Lubavitch USA

☐ Alabama	☐ Louisiana
☐ Arizona	■ Massachusetts
■ California	☐ Maryland
☐ Colorado	☐ Maine
☐ Connecticut	☐ Michigan
☐ Delaware	☐ Minnesota
■ Florida	☐ Missouri
☐ Georgia	☐ North Carolina
☐ Hawaii	☐ Nebraska
☐ Iowa	☐ New Jersey
☐ Illinois	■ New York
☐ Indiana	☐ Ohio
☐ Kentucky	☐ Oklahoma

Oregon	Texas
Pennsylvania	Virginia
Rhode Island	Vermont
South Carolina	Washington
Tennessee	Wisconsin

Photo (upper right, page 130): Conference On Small and Remote Communities, October 1988, Brooklyn, N.Y. The rabbis and rabbinical students convened to discuss their just-completed visitation programs to small, remote communities around the globe. They were joined at the conference by a four-man panel representing 74 small communities in the U.S. and Canada.
 From left to right, seated: (Countries visited are indicated in parentheses.) Yehudah Shemtov, Sholom Ber Minkowitz (Japan; Korea; Hong Kong; Bangkok, Thailand; Singapore; Bombay, India). Mendel Block, Yonah Shur (Berlin, Germany). Chaim Springer, Mendel Feigenson (Aruba; Curacao, Netherland Antilles).
 Rabbi Yehudah Krinsky (Secretariat of the Rebbe), Rabbi Moshe Kotlarsky (Merkos L'Inyonei Chinuch).

Scotland

England

Holland
Belgium

Austria
France Switzerland

Italy

Spain

Tunisia

Morocco

Israel

Hong Kong

Australia

South Africa

Chabad-Lubavitch International

- Argentina
- Australia
- Austria
- Belgium
- Brazil
- Canada
- Chile
- Colombia
- England
- France
- Holland
- Hong Kong
- Israel
- Italy
- Morocco
- Panama
- Paraguay
- Peru
- Scotland
- South Africa
- Spain
- Switzerland
- Tunisia
- Uruguay
- Venezuela

Dovid Polter, Moshe Silver (Virgin Islands; Puerto Rico). Yehoshua Harlig, Yisroel Mangel (Denmark; Sweden; Finland). Zalman Karp (Mexico). Shlomo Ben Tulila, Meyer Shmuckler (Abidjan, Ivory Coast; Nairobi, Kenya; Niger, Nigeria; Cameroon, Kinshasa, Zaire).

Standing left to right: Yaakov Sachs, Mendel Bogomilsky (Venezuela; Bolivia; Peru; Ecuador; Colombia). Mendel Begun (Panama; Costa Rica; Guatemala). Yosef Kirshenbaum, Yecheskel Tanis (23 cities in the interior of Argentina). Naftali Rottenstriech, Zalman Shmotkin (Hawaiian Islands). Moshe Drizin, Shmuel Kaminetsky (Frankfurt, Germany). Mendel Shemtov, Avrohom Holtzberg, Pinchos Sheiner, Dovid Simon (Representatives of seventy four shluchim from small communities in the United States and Canada).

**In Honor Of
The Rebbe
*Sh'lita***

לזכות

כ"ק אדמו"ר שליט"א

ויה"ר שיראה הרבה נחת משלוחיו, תלמידיו, חסידיו, ומכלל ישראל ויניהיג את כולנו מתוך בריאות מלאה, הרחבה ונחת, ובקרוב ממש נלך, כל בנ"י שליט"א, קוממיות לארצנו הקדושה

May it be Hashem's will that the Rebbe *sh'lita* derive much *nachass* from his *sh'luchim,*

his *talmidim* and his chassidim as well as from all Israel. May he continue to lead us all in perfect

health, and may the entire Jewish nation be speedily taken to the Holy Land, with the coming

of our righteous *Mashiach.*

◆　　◆　　◆

נדפס ע"י
הרה"ת **יוסף יצחק** הכהן שי' וזוג' מרת **שטערנא מרים** תחי'
בניהם : **שרה רבקה, מרדכי זאב** הכהן, **זלמן שמעון** הכהן, **חי' שצערא, איסר אשר** הכהן, **זהבה**
שיחיו לאורך ימים ושנים טובות
גוטניק
שנת תִּשְׂמַח וְתִשַׂמַח — שנת הקהל

Dedicated by

The Gutnick Family

Rabbi Yosef Yitschak, his wife Shterna Miriam, and their children—

Sara Rivka, Mordechai Z'ev Hakohen, Zalman Shimon Hakohen, Chaya Shtzera, Isser Asher Hakohen,

Zahava—they should all live long, blessed, good years.